BRITISH AND IRISH
LIONS
PLAYER BY PLAYER

First published in the UK in 2013

© Demand Media Limited 2013

www.demand-media.co.uk

Printed and bound in China.

ISBN 978-1-909217-28-7

The views in this book are those of the author but they are general views only and readers are urged to consult the relevant and qualified specialist for individual advice in particular situations. Demand Media Limited hereby exclude all liability to the extent permitted by law of any errors or omissions in this book and for any loss, damage or expense (whether direct or indirect) suffered by a third party relying on any information contained in this book.

CONTENTS

4		Foreword
6	A	Ackford, Andrew
8	B	Back, Bassett, Beaumont, Bebb, Bennett, Bentley, Brown, Bush, Butterfield
18	C	Calder, Campbell, Campbell-Lamerton, Colclough, Cotton, Crean
25	D	Dallaglio, Davidson, Davies, Davies, Dawes, Dawson, Dawson, Dooley, Duckham, Duggan
38	E	Edwards, Evans
41	G	Gibbs, Gibson, Greenwood, Greenwood, Guscott
47	H	Hastings, Hewitt, Hill, Howley
51	I	Irvine
52	J	Jackson, Jeeps, Jenkins, John, John, Johnson, Jones, Jones, Jones,
62	K	Kiernan, Kyle
64	L	Laidlaw, Leonard
67	M	Matthews, McBride, McGeechan, McLauchlan, McLeod, McLoughlin, Meredith, Meredith, Millar, Moore, Morgan, Mullen
81	N	Nicholls
82	O	O'Callaghan, O'Connell, O'Driscoll, O'Reilly
86	P	Pask, Price, Pullin
89	Q	Quinnell
90	R	Richards, Robinson, Rodber
95	S	Scotland, Shaw, Slattery, Smith, Smith, Squire
101	T	Taylor, Teague, Telfer, Thomas
105	U	Underwood, Uttley
108	V	Vickery
109	W	Wheeler, Wilkinson, Williams, Williams, Williams, Williams, Williams, Windsor, Winterbottom, Wood
123	Y	Young

Foreword

Before I played the first Test against South Africa on the Lions tour in 1997, I remember driving on the bus to Newlands in Cape Town. All along the road and on the lampposts were pictures of lions being strangled by springboks, and there were lines of South African supporters expecting carnage. The fear of failure immediately became the biggest motivation for me on that tour, and, when you factored in our desire for success, you had an explosive mix.

Some members of the English media, such as Stephen Jones from The Sunday Times, were quite negative about the non-English selections (despite the fact that he is Welsh!) and I was extremely aware that two Irishmen (Paul Wallace and Keith Wood) and a Scot in the front row would be in the firing line if things went wrong. I know the Springbok pack were also pleased that we were a small front three because they believed they could overpower us. What we lacked in size, we had to make up in technique. Our series victory proved that we could compete with the best in the world.

A Lions tour is a unique and special event. I hope you enjoy this list of the 100 greatest players to pull on the famous red jersey.

Tom Smith
2013

Ackford

Above: Paul Ackford #4 of the British Lions wrestles with Tim Gavin of the Anzacs

England team–mate Jeremy Guscott said that former police officer Paul Ackford was the best lock he'd ever played with. Ackford was a late developer and only made it into the full England team at the age of 30, a decade after playing for the England B side while still at Cambridge. At 6'7" he was a formidable presence in the scrum and lineout, and his handling skills and big-match temperament made him an asset to any side.

When he finally broke into the England team in 1988, he formed a formidable partnership with fellow policeman Wade Dooley. They were both selected for the 1989 Lions tour of Australia, where, along with Mike Teague, they helped pick the Lions up after defeat in the first Test and then drove the forwards to victory in the last two Tests to seal the series win.

Ackford will also be remembered for being knocked out by 18-year-old Argentinean prop Federico Mendez at Twickenham in 1990. Mendez had been stamped on in a ruck by Jeff Probyn but he misidentified the culprit and caught Ackford with a disgraceful blindside shot, for which he was dismissed.

Ackford's consistency and commitment made him an England regular for the next two seasons and he played a central role in their 1991 Grand Slam. His international career came to an end following England's 12-6 defeat to Australia in the 1991 World Cup final, although

serial England-baiter David Campese paid him the ultimate compliment when he said: "This guy was tough and durable, a real workhorse in the pack. It's a shame he was a Pom and not an Aussie."

Ackford now has a column in the *Sunday Telegraph*.

Name: Paul John Ackford
Born: 26th February 1958, Hanover, West Germany
Home Union: England
Position: Lock
Height / Weight: 6'7" (2.00m) / 250lbs (112kg)
Lions Tours: Australia (1989)
Number of Tests: 3
Points: 0

Andrew

One of England's greatest fly-halves, Rob Andrew was a master tactician and formidable kicker, which helped him become one of his country's highest scorers. He only became England's dead-ball specialist in 1994, however, but he immediately upped his average from three points a game to 15.

Although a talented cricketer who captained Cambridge University and scored a century against Nottinghamshire in 1984, he made his oval-ball debut for England against Romania in 1985 and scored 18 of England's 22 points. He was inconsistent for the next few seasons but by 1989 he was the first-choice fly-half and earned a late call-up for the Lions tour to Australia.

In 1993 he claimed the No.10 shirt for the tour of New Zealand but, despite winning the second Test to level the series, the Lions couldn't compete with the Kiwis in their own backyard and lost the deciding rubber.

Under Will Carling, Andrew became a Grand Slam winner three times – in 1991, 1992 and 1995 – as well as making it to the final of the 1991 World Cup, although England narrowly lost to Australia. He had his revenge in 1995, however, when his last-gasp drop-goal put out the defending champions after an epic quarter-final. The side was eventually put to the sword by a Jonah Lomu-inspired New Zealand in the semis and finished fourth overall.

Andrew received a lot of criticism for kicking too much but this was one of English rugby's most successful periods and he was working behind one of the most destructive packs in the game. He scored more than 20 points in a game seven times and became the first Englishman to complete a personal grand slam when scoring a try, drop goal, five penalties and two conversions against South Africa in 1994.

When the game turned professional in 1995, he left Wasps and became player and director of rugby at Newcastle Falcons. Here he oversaw the development of many young players, most notably Jonny Wilkinson. In the 1997-98 season Andrew led the Falcons to the premiership title and two English Cup victories.

In 2006 he became the RFU's Elite Rugby Director. His first job was to sack England coach Andy Robinson in favour of Brian Ashton.

Above: *Rob Andrew*

Name: Christopher Robert 'Rob' Andrew, MBE
Born: 18th February 1963, Richmond, Yorkshire
Home Union: England
Position: Fly-half
Height / Weight: 5'9" (1.75m) / 180lbs (82kg)
Lions Tours: Australia (1989), New Zealand (1993)
Number of Tests: 5
Points: 11

Back

A master of controlling the ball in a rolling maul, a defensive guru, and another pivotal player in the World Cup-winning team of 2003, Neil Back almost didn't measure up to the job. They say size doesn't matter but for years Back was considered too small for international rugby. He'd tried to cut it as a scrum-half but then decided to follow in the footsteps of hero Jean-Pierre Rives and make it as a top-drawer flanker.

His hard work and sheer bloody-mindedness paid off and he made his England debut against Scotland in 1994. Two years later he showed his fiery side when he pushed over referee Steve Lander after the Pilkington Cup final and earned himself a six-month ban. In 2002, Leicester were in danger of losing to Munster in the Heineken Cup when Back swatted the ball from Peter Stringer's hand before a scrum in the dying minutes deep in the Leicester 22. The referee and officials missed the incident, and Leicester cleared their lines and eventually won 15-9.

He bounced back from this low point and his ferocious tackling and unrivalled fitness earned him a call-up to the Lions squad to tour South Africa in 1997 (and an RFU player-of-the-year nomination in 1998). He came on in the decisive second Test at King's Park in Durban and helped the Lions to the unlikeliest of series wins against the then world champions.

Back, Dallaglio and Richard Hill then formed the most-capped back row in the history of the game and they drove the England side to new heights. Between 1999 and 2002, he also enjoyed phenomenal success with club Leicester, winning four successive Zurich Premiership titles and ending 1999 as the club's top try scorer with 16. His form saw him called up for the 2001 Lions tour to Australia and he duly delivered, scoring a try in the second Test. Sadly the team could not build on a big win in the first game and they eventually lost the series 2-1.

Back famously vowed never to retire from international rugby and he was an integral part of the 2003 England side that won the World Cup in Australia. He did finally retire from the national set-up after the 2004 Six Nations however but, at 36, he was a surprise inclusion in the squad for the 2005 Lions tour to New Zealand but the side didn't perform and his international career came to an end.

There's no doubt that Back helped rewrite the way an open-side flanker should play and he brought a fitness and energy to sides that has since become the norm. He enjoyed a brief stint as Leicester's defensive coach before joining National League Three side Rugby Lions.

Name: Neil Antony Back, MBE
Born: 16th January 1969, Coventry
Home Union: England
Position: Flanker
Height / Weight: 5'10" (1.78m) / 210lbs (93kg)
Lions Tours: South Africa (1997), Australia (2001), New Zealand (2005)
Number of Tests: 5
Points: 5

Left: *Neil Back (right) and Martin Johnson of the British and Irish Lions combine to tackle Toutai Kefu of Australia*

Bassett

Right: *John Bassett, Wales Captain*

Bassett's rugby career began with Kenfig Hill and Pyle but, having joined the police, he played for the Constabulary and Penarth. In 1928, the national selectors were looking for a dependable full-back and Bassett was chosen to represent his country after a one-off game against Newport.

He earned his first international cap against England the following year, and by 1930 he'd been appointed captain of Wales. He enjoyed a great start to the 1930 Five Nations and single-handedly saved his side against Ireland. He would have taken the field against the French but he'd already been called up for the British Lions and was on his way to Australia.

He had an exceptional tour, outplaying local favourite George Nepia in the tourists' four matches against New Zealand, and was immediately proclaimed the best full-back in world rugby. He played in five Test matches on the tour and his powerful defence often turned ball over for the Lions to use in attack. When he returned home he immediately guided Wales to their first home nations' championship in a decade.

He was criticised for his poor tactics against the touring South Africans in 1931 but he retained the captaincy and helped Wales win their first two matches in the 1932 Five Nations. Then the wheels fell off, however. He dropped a high ball and gifted Ireland a try, then missed a tackle to allow the Irish in for a second score. The Triple Crown could still have been sealed had Bassett kicked a last-minute conversion but he missed, thus ending his international career.

Name: John Archibald 'Jack' Bassett
Born: 11th July 1905, Trebanog
Died: 19th February 1989, Cardiff
Home Union: Wales
Position: Full-back
Height / Weight: 5'10" (1.78m) / 189lbs (86kg)
Lions Tours: Australia & New Zealand (1930)
Number of Tests: 5
Points: 0

Beaumont

England has been blessed with several inspirational leaders over the last 30 years, none more so than Bill Beaumont. The big lock could motivate a team with common sense, a friendly demeanour and example-setting performances.

Beaumont was a one-club man with Fylde, made his England debut in 1975 when he came on in the last minute against Ireland in Dublin for the injured Roger Uttley, and was soon a regular in the national set-up. His power around the park and clean takes in the lineout saw him called up halfway through the 1977 Lions tour of New Zealand when Nigel Horton broke his thumb. He didn't disappoint and immediately formed a strong second-row partnership with Gordon Brown in the final three Tests. The Lions should have shared the series 2-2 but conceded a late try in the fourth match.

Beaumont was given the England captaincy in 1978, and he guided the side to a historic Grand Slam in 1980. He then became the first Englishman to lead the Lions in half a century when he was selected as captain for the 1980 tour to South Africa. The side may have lost the first three Tests, but the matches were incredibly close and the Lions salvaged some pride with a 17-13 win in the final Test at Loftus Versfeld in Pretoria. They also won all of their 14 matches against the provincial sides.

Beaumont was awarded an OBE in 1982

Above: *Bill Beaumont in action against South Africa*

but a head injury in the County Championship final brought his career to a premature end later that year. He promptly took over as a team captain on A Question of Sport before joining the International Rugby Board. He also helped manage the unsuccessful Lions tour of New Zealand in 2005. In 2007, the County Championship competition was renamed the Bill Beaumont Cup in his honour.

Name: William Blackledge 'Bill' Beaumont, CBE
Born: 9th March 1952, Chorley, Lancashire
Home Union: England
Position: Lock
Height / Weight: 6'3" (1.91m) / 226lbs (103kg)
Lions Tours: New Zealand (1977), South Africa (1980)
Number of Tests: 7
Points: 0

Bebb

The son of Welsh historian Ambrose Bebb, Dewi was educated at Friars School and Trinity College, Carmarthen. He was a talented and pacey wing who made his first-team debut for Swansea against Llanelli in 1958. In all,

he would make 221 appearances for the club, scoring 87 tries and captaining them for two seasons, 1963-65.

He won the first of his 34 caps for Wales against England in 1959. Having proved himself a potent try-scoring winger, he was selected for Wales's first overseas tour in 1964, although he'd already been abroad with the Lions in South Africa two years previously. The tourists won 16 of their 25 games but lost three of the four Tests.

In 1966 Bebb was again asked to tour with the Lions. The Australian leg went to plan and the tourists won five of six provincial matches and hammered the hosts in both Tests. But the New Zealanders were a much tougher proposition and the Lions lost all three Tests against the All Blacks. They did manage to beat Canada in Toronto on the way home, however.

He retired from the game in 1967 and became a successful broadcaster and journalist.

Name: Dewi Iorwerth Ellis Bebb
Born: 7th August 1938, Bangor
Died: 14th March 1996, Pontypridd
Home Union: Wales
Position: Wing
Lions Tours: South Africa (1962), Australia & New Zealand (1966)
Number of Tests: 8
Points: 3

Bennett

Bennett had a superb sidestep, searing change of pace and a dazzling array of skills that would see him become one of the best-loved players of his generation. At the age of just 20 he became the first substitute for Wales when he came on in Paris for the injured Gerald Davies. He occasionally played at centre or full-back but, when the great Barry John retired, he made the fly-half position his own.

Bennett's supreme skills were showcased at the legendary game between the Barbarians and the All Blacks in Cardiff in 1973, and it was he who sidestepped four opponents before launching the famous counterattack that saw Gareth Edwards score the best try in the game's history. (He'd previously masterminded Llanelli's epic win over the All Blacks.)

In what was fast-becoming a golden age for Welsh rugby, Bennett was a shoe-in for the 1974 Lions tour to South Africa and he didn't disappoint, scoring more than a hundred points and obliterating the hosts' defence with a 50-yard solo run in Pretoria. The tour was a resounding success and the Lions won 21 of 22 matches, with a solitary draw in the final Test, and they restricted the physically imposing South Africans to just 34 points in the four matches.

On the domestic front, competition for places meant that Bennett was dropped in 1975 but he returned to the national team the following year and took over as captain from Mervyn Davies. Welsh rugby was still the dominant force in Europe so he was also selected to captain the 1977 Lions tour to New Zealand. Of their 26 matches, they won 21 and lost five, but that included three of the four Tests against the hosts. It was series they should have drawn but they conceded a last-minute score in the decisive fourth Test that swayed the series in New Zealand's favour. The side also lost a Test match in Fiji on the way home, 25-21, although they did beat the Barbarians at Twickenham as part of the queen's silver jubilee celebrations.

He retired in 1978, was inducted into the International Rugby Hall of Fame in 2005 and the Welsh Sports Hall of Fame two years later.

Name: Phil Bennett, OBE
Born: 24th October 1948, Felinfoel
Home Union: Wales
Position: Fly-half
Height / Weight: 5'7" (1.71m) / 163lbs (74kg)
Lions Tours: South Africa (1974), New Zealand (1977)
Number of Tests: 8
Points: 44

Bentley

Bentley was a talented athlete who first played rugby union with Sale and was capped by England against Ireland in 1988. He also toured against Australia later that year and looked set to become a regular fixture in Will Carling's side. But then he decided that he'd rather play professionally so he quit his job as a policeman and joined rugby league side Leeds before moving to Halifax in 1992.

When rugby union turned professional in 1995, Bentley was lured back by the Newcastle Falcons and he caused such a stir that he was a surprise selection for the 1997 Lions tour to South Africa. He was expected to be a fringe player but he left five Gauteng tacklers in his wake on his way to a magnificent solo try for the mid-week side and was drafted in for the second Test. Although his defence occasionally let him down, he marshalled opposite number James Small well and the Lions secured their historic series win.

He played twice more for England before returning to league outfit Huddersfield Giants. He now runs training camps and is a regular on the after-dinner circuit.

Name: John Bentley
Born: 5th September 1966, Dewsbury, Yorkshire
Home Union: England
Position: Wing
Height / Weight: 6'0" (1.83m) / 216lbs (98kg)
Lions Tours: 1997
Number of Tests: 2
Points: 0

Brown

Gordon Brown was from solid sporting stock: his father played in goal for Scotland and his brother also played rugby for their country. He won the first of his 30 Scotland caps against South Africa in 1969 and retained his place in the next Five Nations Championship. He was selected for the 1971 tour to the 'land of the long white cloud' and played his way into the Test side with typical gusto. He needed 20 stitches after being punched but, despite the bloodshed, enjoyed perhaps his best game in the red shirt during the second Test.

He became a giant among mortals in the story of the Lions, physically and in spirit, when he was partnered with Willie John McBride in the engine room on the 1974 South Africa tour. The cornerstone of the pack, he scored eight tries in 12 matches, a record for a lock. Two of his tries came in the internationals and were crucial to the Lions' 3-0 defeat of the Springboks. He was also an integral part of the team off the field and his team talks became the stuff of legend (he would later enjoy great success on the after-dinner speaking circuit).

He returned to New Zealand in 1977 even though he'd retired from Scottish international duty and was again the outstanding forward. He died from cancer in 2001.

Name: Gordon Lamont Brown
Born: 1st November 1947, Troon
Died: 19th March 2001, Troon
Home Union: Scotland
Position: Lock
Height / Weight: 6'5" (1.97m) / 225lbs (103kg)
Lions Tours: New Zealand (1971), South Africa (1974), New Zealand (1977)
Tests: 8
Points: 0

Above: *Scotland's Gordon Brown (centre, right) and Wales's Dai Morris (centre, left) fail to reach the ball at a line out*

Bush

Bush was a Cardiff RFC stalwart and eventually racked up more than 170 appearances for the club, as well as being appointed captain. He only won eight caps for his country but he will be forever remembered as being in the side that beat the 1905 All Blacks.

The previous year, Bush had been selected to tour Australia and New Zealand with the British Isles and he played in all four Tests. He was so skilful and elusive that the Australian media christened him Will o' the Wisp, and the tourists dispatched the hosts comfortably in every game. The second phase of the tour was more difficult and, despite winning their opening two games in New Zealand, they then lost the all-important Test match. Overall, however, the tour was well-received by the hosts and the matches were covered extensively in the media. Despite being a relatively new institution, the Lions were off to a good start.

One of the most talented Welshmen of the pre-war era, Bush was also an accomplished cricketer.

Name: Percy Frank Bush
Born: 23rd June 1879, Cardiff
Died: 19th May 1955, Cardiff
Home Union: Wales
Position: Fly-half
Lions Tours: Australia & New Zealand (1904)
Number of Tests: 4
Points: 20

Butterfield

Born in Yorkshire, Butterfield's style of play at school was influenced by the more expansive game of rugby league. He was also a top athlete and swimmer at Cleckheaton grammar school before he went to Loughborough to develop his all-round skills. His rugby career blossomed at Northampton, where he made 227 appearances, and he was also selected to play for Yorkshire in the County Championship. He represented the county 54 times and was captain from 1951 to 1958.

When Butterfield forced his way into the England team, he became such a regular fixture that he played in a record 28 successive Tests from 1953 to 1959. He helped the side to a Grand Slam in 1957 – their first for 29 years – and this provided the springboard for his two tours with the Lions, the first of which was the 1955 trip to South Africa. This series would see his reputation grow and he was instrumental in the side's two wins, although South Africa fought back well and won the last Test to draw the rubber.

Butterfield scored tries in three of the four Tests and he and Wales's Cliff Morgan were all but untouchable. He was the ideal centre and his individual skills and consistency made him one of England's greatest players. Where others called on brawn, Butterfield relied on subtlety and sublime handling, the first prince of centres in the British Isles.

Butterfield was named England captain for the 1959 Five Nations Championship and he was again selected for the Lions tour to New Zealand later that year. He picked up an injury, however, and didn't make the Test side. He retired in the early 1960s suffering from arthritis. He then helped pen the first RFU coaching manuals and often hosted events at The Rugby Club in Hallam Street, London. Although ill health removed him from the public eye, he was President of Milton Keynes RFC until his death in 2004.

Above: *Jeff Butterfield.*

Name: Jeffrey Butterfield
Born: 9th August 1929, Heckmondwike, Yorkshire
Died: 30th April 2004, Wicken, Northamptonshire
Home Union: England
Position: Centre
Height / Weight: 5'11" (1.81m) / 196lbs (89kg)
Lions Tours: South Africa (1955), New Zealand (1959)
Number of Tests: 4
Points: 12

Calder

Right: *Ian McGeechan (right) reassures captain Finlay Calder*

Finlay Calder learned his trade as a combative and destructive open-side flanker at Stewart's Melville College, but it was brother Jim who first appeared for the national team. The elder of the two earned his last cap against Wales in 1985 and Finlay took up the family mantle aged 29 when he was called up for the first of his 34 caps in a 1986 Five Nations encounter with France.

Just three years later, Calder was selected as captain for the Lions' tour to Australia, the first time they'd been back to the country since 1971. The Lions were poor in the first Test and lost 30-12, their heaviest defeat to Australia. But with England's Mike Teague recovered from injury, the forwards were far more influential in the second Test and they won what was basically a glorified fight 19-12 in Brisbane. They then scraped home 19-18 in the series decider after David Campese tried to break out from behind his own line and ended up gifting the tourists a try. It was the low point of the mercurial winger's career and it still haunts him today. They hadn't beaten the Lions at that point and Campese was severely criticised in the media. Calder therefore became the first man to win a series having gone 1-0 down.

He carried on playing until Scotland were beaten by Australia at the 1991 World Cup, with his greatest moment coming at Murrayfield in the 1990 Grand Slam decider against England.

The 'auld enemy' were hot favourites to take the honours but the back row of Calder, John Jeffrey and Derek White nullified the English forwards and they scraped home to record a famous 13-7 Calcutta Cup win.

Calder went on to coach Gala and Edinburgh Academicals but now earns his living as a grain merchant.

Name: Finlay Calder
Born: 20th August 1957, Haddington
Home Union: Scotland
Position: Flanker
Lions Tours: Australia (1989)
Number of Tests: 3
Points: 0

Campbell

Hamstring problems hampered Campbell's early career but he still made an impression at Belvedere College and helped his side to the Leinster Schools Senior Cup in 1971 and '72. He first played for Ireland aged 21 in 1976 but he didn't play again until 1979, although he would go on to score 217 points in just 22 internationals.

He enjoyed a successful tour to Australia with the national side in 1979 and this proved to be the springboard to success with the Lions because he was selected for the 1980 trip to South Africa. He played in three Tests having recovered from yet more hamstring troubles, with his first action coming as a replacement during the second Test in Bloemfontein.

Campbell started the third and fourth Tests and was the Lions' leading points' scorer on the tour. His accuracy with the boot and reliable distribution saw him selected again for the 1983 tour to New Zealand but the side was not particularly strong and he only won one of his seven Tests for the tourists. Despite this, Campbell was named one of the New Zealand Rugby Almanac's five players of the year.

His defining moment was helping Ireland to their first Triple Crown in 33 years during the 1982 Five Nations, and they took a share of the championship the following year. As well as kicking all of his side's 21 points in the match that secured the Triple Crown, Campbell set an

Left: *Ollie Campbell kicks three of his 22 points against Western Province on the 1980 tour to South Africa*

Irish record on their tour to Australia three years earlier when he scored 60 points.

Campbell retired from international rugby in 1984 and from all rugby two years later. He has since worked as a company director in the family clothing business.

Name: Seamus Oliver 'Ollie' Campbell
Born: 5th March 1954, Dublin
Home Union: Ireland
Position: Fly-half
Height / Weight: 5'10" (1.78m) / 169lbs (77kg)
Lions Tours: South Africa (1980), New Zealand (1983)
Number of Tests: 7
Points: 26

Campbell-Lamerton

Below: *Mike Campbell-Lamerton*

Campbell-Lamerton was born in Malta but went to school near Windsor. He was struck in the chest with a javelin on the playing fields but somehow survived – it wouldn't be his only brush with death, however. After his national service he joined the army and served in Korea and Cyprus. Whilst in the Far East he trod on a mine but a colleague rendered it safe before it went off. Three years later he fell 60 feet from a helicopter in full combat gear and suffered serious back and leg injuries.

He used his downtime in the army to play rugby and made his Scotland debut against France in 1961, and he was a regular in the team for the next five years. This brought him to the attention of the Lions selectors and he was picked for the 1962 South Africa tour. The physically-imposing Scotsman played all four matches at Number 8. The tourists drew the first match, then lost the next two narrowly before being comprehensively outplayed in the fourth Test.

Campbell-Lamerton was chosen to lead the 1966 party on their tour of Australia and New Zealand. He played in the second row in both Tests against the Wallabies, which the tourists won 11-8 and 31-0, but, after the opening match against the All Blacks – a heavy 20-3 loss – Campbell-Lamerton relinquished the captaincy to David Watkins for the second and fourth Tests because he felt he wasn't playing well enough. It was the gesture of a man who was putting the team first and it endeared him to team-mates and the media.

Despite missing out in two of the four Tests, he fulfilled the team's media commitments by making 257 speeches and more than 100 television and radio interviews. He was credited with being the glue that held the tour party together on what was a difficult and much-criticised trip.

Campbell-Lamerton died in 2005 after a long battle with prostate cancer.

Name: Colonel Michael John 'Mike' Campbell-Lamerton
Born: 1st August 1933, Malta
Died: 17th March 2005
Home Union: Scotland
Position: Lock, Number 8
Height / Weight: 6'5" (1.96m) / 252lbs (113kg)
Lions Tours: South Africa (1962), Australia & New Zealand (1966)
Number of Tests: 7
Points: 3

Colclough

As one of the locks in England's Grand Slam-winning side of 1980, Maurice Colclough wasn't known for his try-scoring, but in 1983 he bulldozed over the line against New Zealand for one of the most famous tries in English rugby history. It was his only international score in his 25 England matches between 1978 and 1986, and it helped his side record a 15-9 win.

Born in Oxford, Colclough was educated at the Duke of York's Royal Military School, Dover, and Liverpool University, playing for Liverpool RFC. He also played for Kent and London Schools, Sussex and Lancashire, and for London against Argentina and New Zealand. His performances saw him selected for the 1980 Lions tour to South Africa but he couldn't use his huge frame as an advantage over the hosts and the tourists narrowly lost the first three Tests. A win in the final Test of a dead rubber couldn't paper over the cracks.

His domestic career was on the up however, and he was an influential player in the historic Grand Slam season of 1980. He was also one of the first Englishmen to captain a French provincial side and earned a reputation as a practical joker, once convincing team-mate Colin (not so) Smart to drink aftershave following a victory over the French.

Colclough was a powerful and athletic figure in the second row and his continued presence in the England setup saw him tour to New Zealand in 1983. Again, the Lions narrowly lost the first three matches, but they were hammered in the fourth and drew deserved criticism from the fans and media. Colclough's performances saw him return home in credit, however.

He retired from international rugby in 1986 but died in 2006 from a brain tumour.

> **Name:** Maurice John Colclough
> **Born:** 2nd September 1953, Oxford
> **Died:** 27th January 2006
> **Home Union:** England
> **Position:** Lock
> **Height / Weight:** 6'5" (1.96m) / 248lbs (112kg)
> **Lions Tours:** South Africa (1980), New Zealand (1983)
> **Number of Tests:** 8
> **Points:** 0

Above: *Maurice Colclough (right) with team mate, and England Rugby Union captain, Billy Beaumont*

Cotton

Cotton was born in Wigan and studied physical education at Loughborough. He was soon making a name for himself as a combative prop and he made his first appearance for England in the 1971 Calcutta Cup match against Scotland.

His physical presence was needed on the 1974 Lions tour to South Africa but the piano shifters – as the front five forwards are often known – rarely get as much praise as the piano players in the backs. Fran Cotton, however, ensured that the formidable South African forwards were ineffective and the tour was a huge success.

Cotton honed his craft in a struggling England team but they eventually came good in 1980. He was also on hand to give the Kiwis a run for their money during the 1977 tour – this time as a tight-head prop – but the visitors were generally outplayed and, although they competed upfront, didn't have the flair or creativity in the backline to finish off promising moves. During the tour, Cotton became the subject of one of sport's most famous images, The Muddy Man, when Colorsport's Colin Elsey pictured him caked in dirt at a lineout. He would have played a part in the return to South Africa in 1980 but a health scare cut his tour short.

Cotton retired from rugby to concentrate on working for the Wooden Spoon Society but he still made an all-time Test team selected by legendary commentator Bill McLaren. His retirement was blighted by a ban after writing his autobiography, which in the eyes of the rugby establishment classed him as a professional, but that didn't stop him committing himself to the management team for the Lions on their historic tour to South Africa in 1997. He made a huge contribution and was highly praised for the side's series win. He was also a key figure in the appointment of Clive Woodward as England coach.

In 2005 Cotton resigned from the RFU to concentrate on his businesses. He again backed Woodward the following year as the latter pitched for a role as the RFU's Elite Rugby Director but Rob Andrew beat Woodward to the job.

Cotton founded Cotton Traders with former England team-mate Steve Smith in 1987. The business now employs 600 staff across the UK and turns over in excess of £50 million annually.

Name: Francis Edward Cotton
Born: 3rd January 1947, Wigan
Home Union: England
Position: Prop
Height / Weight: 6'2" (1.88m) / 231lbs (105kg)
Lions Tours: South Africa (1974), New Zealand (1977), South Africa (1980)
Number of Tests: 7
Points: 0

Right: *Thomas Crean VC*

CREAN

Crean

Crean and his brothers all attended the famous rugby hotbed Belvedere College in Dublin. He developed into a fine all-round athlete but was particularly good at the longer sprints, swimming (he once helped save a fellow student from drowning) and rugby. He then graduated to the Royal College of Surgeons and played throughout his medical career, usually at half-back.

He then switched to the forwards and his game improved to the point where he was selected for Leinster in 1894. In the next three years he made nine appearances and scored two tries for Ireland, helping the side to a Triple Crown in his first season and two more Home Union Championships.

He was one of a number of Irishmen selected for the 1896 tour to South Africa. He played in all four Tests against the hosts and scored a try in the second match of the series. Crean was so influential that he took over as captain for the last two matches, and the British Isles eventually won the series 3-1.

Crean and team-mate Robert Johnston remained in South Africa after the tour and fought in the Second Boer War. Both men were subsequently awarded the highest military honour, the Victoria Cross, for their bravery in battle. Crean's citation remarked that he had tended to two wounded men and a fellow officer while under heavy enemy fire, this despite him being shot in the arm and stomach.

He again served with distinction during the First World War, and was on hand once more to save a jockey's life by removing bone splinters from his brain with nothing more than a hammer and chisel after a fall at Ascot. Declining health forced him to close his Harley Street practice and he died from diabetes at the comparatively young age of 49 in 1923.

Name: Major Dr Thomas Joseph Crean, VC
Born: 19th April 1873, Dublin
Died: 25th March 1923, London
Home Union: Ireland
Position: Forward
Height / Weight: 6'2" (1.87m) / 203lbs (92kg)
Lions Tours: South Africa (1896)
Number of Tests: 4
Points: 3

Dallaglio

As a member of his school choir, Dallaglio famously sang backing vocals on Tina Turner's We Don't Need Another Hero in 1985. Thankfully he chose rugby as a career instead. He had the option to choose whether to play for his father's country of birth, Italy, or indeed his mother's country, Ireland, but he opted for the Red Rose and never looked back.

Dallaglio was an accomplished player at Ampleforth but he lacked discipline and never looked likely to break into the top tier even after he joined Wasps. But in 1993 he was selected for England's World Cup Sevens squad and they surprised everyone by winning the tournament.

(Dallaglio and team-mate Dawson remain the only two players to have won the World Cup in both versions of the game.) He was then asked to tour South Africa with England but he didn't play in the Test series.

Despite not being a regular in the Wasps back row, Rob Andrew and Dean Ryan left for Newcastle with four more players and Dallaglio was suddenly propelled into the top-flight as club captain. He also received his full England call-up in 1995. He led club side Wasps to the first professional English title in 1996 and was then selected for the crucial 1997 Lions tour to South Africa.

He was a regular fixture in the victorious team and Clive Woodward rewarded him with the England captaincy later that year. But his

Left: *Dallaglio, the Lions number Eight, charges forward*

tenure as leader of the national team was dogged by injury and controversy, and he was forced to resign the captaincy in the run-up to the 1999 World Cup after an off-field sting by a British tabloid newspaper revealed that he had claimed to have taken recreational drugs, although he countered by saying he had been lying to fit in socially with the reporters.

Martin Johnson took over but Dallaglio remained a massive presence in the back row alongside Neil Back and Richard Hill. It is a testament to both his resilience and his ability that he was given back the Wasps and England captaincy in 2000 while Johnson was out. In 2001, as part of the Lions squad, he suffered a career-threatening knee injury but he silenced

the doubters who claimed he was past his best by returning fitter and stronger.

Between 2003 and 2005 Wasps dominated the Premiership, winning the title three times. In 2004 they also conquered Europe, beating Toulouse in the last minute of the Heineken Cup final. Dallaglio was also an integral member of England's Grand Slam and World Cup-winning teams in 2003, and he was then awarded the MBE. When Johnson retired, Dallaglio once again took over as captain, although he led a less successful Six Nations campaign and announced his retirement in 2004. Despite this, he was called up for the Lions in 2005 but he fractured an ankle in the first game and missed the rest of the tour. It looked like he would then slide into retirement having achieved just about everything in the sport.

There was one last hurrah, however. Dallaglio announced that he was once again available for international selection in 2005 and he soon added to his 73 caps and 15 tries. In 2007 he made a huge impact from the bench and helped England to yet another World Cup final. Despite coming up just short against the Springboks, Dallaglio cemented his status as one of the game's greatest forwards with a brutal work ethic and giant personality.

Dallaglio now spends his time working for various charities and he has since helped raise more than £10 million. A legend in his own lifetime.

Name: Lorenzo Bruno Nero 'Lawrence' Dallaglio, OBE
Born: 10th August 1972, London
Home Union: England
Position: Flanker, Number 8
Height / Weight: 6'4" (1.93m) / 247lbs (112kg)
Lions Tours: South Africa (1997), Australia (2001), New Zealand (2005)
Number of Tests: 3
Points: 0

Davidson

Davidson was a giant but mobile second-row who began his club career with Dungannon before moving to London Irish and then Castres Olympique. He made his Test debut in Ireland's 44-8 annihilation of Fiji at Lansdowne Road in 1995. He was then selected for the 1997 Lions' tour to South Africa and was omnipresent in the engine room. His partnership with Martin Johnson was one of the reasons the Springboks got no change from the Lions pack, and he was equally proficient at the set-piece to deny the hosts lineout ball. Davidson was voted the players' player of the tour.

In 1999 he played three matches for Ireland at the World Cup and made his final appearance in the green jersey at Murrayfield in 2001, although Ireland were hammered 32-10. He was selected for the Lions tour of Australia later that year but couldn't reach the heights of South Africa and didn't play in any of the Tests.

He finished his career with 32 caps after aggravating an old injury and has since enjoyed stints as Director of Rugby at Dungannon and as a coach at Castres. In 2009 he joined the coaching staff at Ulster.

Left: *Ireland's Jeremy Davidson*

Name: Jeremy Davidson
Born: 28th April 1974, Belfast
Home Union: Ireland
Position: Lock
Height / Weight: 6'6" (1.98m) / 252lbs (115kg)
Lions Tours: South Africa (1997)
Number of Tests: 3
Points: 0

Davies, Mervyn

Right: Mervyn Davies of the British Lions in action during the Rugby Lions tour of South Africa

Davies attended Penlan School and was immediately earmarked as a future star. He then played for London Welsh before moving home to join Swansea. He won his first cap for Wales against Scotland at the age of 23 and he soon developed a 'Merv the Swerve' nickname on account of his mazy runs.

He became a permanent fixture at number eight in the Welsh side and racked up 38 consecutive matches, during which he scored two tries. His mastery of the forward game saw him selected for the Lions tours to New Zealand in 1971, where he played all four Tests, and South Africa three years later, where he again played in every Test. The tours were a great success and this was mirrored in his performances for Wales. The national team won two Grand Slams and three Triple Crowns with Davies at the back of the scrum, and in his 46 full internationals he only lost nine times.

His magnificent career was brought to a premature end by a haemorrhage in 1976. In 2001 he was inducted into the International Hall of Fame and the following year he was voted the best Welsh captain and number eight in the country's history, high praise indeed. A heavy smoker, Davies was diagnosed with lung cancer in 2011. The following year the rugby world mourned the loss of one of its greatest exponents.

Name: Thomas Mervyn Davies, OBE
Born: 9th December 1946, Swansea
Died: 15th March 2012
Home Union: Wales
Position: Number 8
Height / Weight: 6'5" (1.95m) / 238lbs (108kg)
Lions Tours: New Zealand (1971), South Africa (1974)
Number of Tests: 8
Points: 0

Davies, Gerald

D avies was a promising schoolboy and was soon plying his trade at Loughborough and Cambridge University. He initially played with Cardiff and London Welsh, and he made his international debut against Argentina at the Arms Park in 1966. He moved from centre to wing for the Welsh tour of New Zealand in 1969, but this was only because he'd played in the position for the 1968 Lions on their tour of South Africa.

Davies was a brilliant running wing who could step off either foot and deliver killer passes from both hands. He cemented his reputation on the 1971 tour to New Zealand and will be forever linked with the all-conquering Welsh sides of the 1970s. His record is virtually unsurpassed: in only 46 internationals for his country he touched down 20 times, and he scored another three tries in five matches for the Lions, all of them on the 1971 tour.

He retired in 1978 after a glittering career and turned his considerable talents to writing for the Times, sitting on the committee to reform Welsh rugby which had entered the doldrums in the 1980s and early 1990s, and devoting time to promoting youth rugby. In 2007 he was appointed to the manager's position for the upcoming Lions tour to South Africa.

Having been soundly beaten in 2005, the Lions needed to roar in 2009 and they didn't disappoint. Although they narrowly lost the first two Test matches, they were titanic encounters and paved the way for a heroic 28-9 win in the third Test in Johannesburg. Had a number of key players not been injured they could well have taken the series – indeed they led deep into injury time in the second Test.

Above: *Gerald Davies of Wales runs with the ball during the Welsh tour to Australia*

> **Name:** Thomas Gerald Reames Davies, CBE
> **Born:** 7th February 1945, Llansaint
> **Home Union:** Wales
> **Position:** Wing
> **Height / Weight:** 5'9" (1.74m) / 163 (74kg)
> **Lions Tours:** South Africa (1968), New Zealand (1971), as a manager: South Africa (2009)
> **Number of Tests:** 5
> **Points:** 9

Dawes

Below: *John Dawes before a Lions tour*

Dawes was educated at Lewis School, the University of Wales and Loughborough. He gained a degree in chemistry and a PGCE, and also played rugby for Newbridge before joining London Welsh.

He won his first international cap against Ireland in 1964 and his performances saw him called up to the touring party of East Africa later the same year. He went on to captain Wales and led them to a Grand Slam in 1971. This pushed him up the pecking order for those being considered for the Lions captaincy, and he was duly appointed before the New Zealand tour. Under the tutelage of Carwyn James, the side became the first – and so far only – Lions team to win a Test series against the All Blacks.

The first match in Dunedin was a tight affair but an Ian McLauchlan try and two penalties saw them scrape home 9-3. Some of the players became overconfident but they were brought down to earth after being on the end of a Kiwi backlash in the second Test. The All Blacks scored five tries to the Lions' two and stormed to a 22-12 victory in Christchurch. The third match in Wellington saw the tourists back to their best and they ran out easy winners, 13-3. If they drew or won the last Test in Auckland, the Lions would seal a historic series win.

It was 8-8 at half-time, with both sides scoring a try, conversion and penalty. And it was 11-11 going into the last 20 minutes when JPR Williams kicked a magnificent 45-metre drop goal, the only one of his career. The All Blacks rallied with a late penalty but could only draw the match.

Dawes followed on from this success by captaining the Barbarians at Cardiff Arms Park when they famously beat New Zealand 23-11 in 1973. He retired the following year and coached the national side until 1979, a period during which Wales won the Five Nations Championship four times. He also coached the Lions on their tour back to New Zealand in 1977, although this trip wasn't as successful.

He is now President of London Welsh and holds the distinction of never having lost to England, either as a player or coach, in his entire career.

Name: Sydney John Dawes, OBE
Born: 29th June 1940, Newbridge
Home Union: Wales
Position: Centre
Height / Weight: 5'10" (1.78m) / 180lbs (82kg)
Lions Tours: New Zealand (1971), and as coach: New Zealand (1977)
Number of Tests: 4
Points: 0

Dawson, Matthew

Dawson was a sporting all-rounder at school. He played cricket for Buckinghamshire U-18s and appeared on the wing for Chelsea Schoolboys. He then decided to switch to the oval-ball game and joined Northampton RFC in 1991, but rugby was still an amateur game so he worked as a security guard and coached in his spare time. He was selected as part of England's un-fancied sevens squad at the inaugural World Cup in Scotland in 1993, but the team raised a few eyebrows by beating Serevi's Fiji and Campese's Australia on their way to a historic win.

He made his international debut in 1995 against Western Samoa and was soon making a case for his inclusion on the Lions tour to South Africa. He left the UK as the side's third choice scrum-half behind Robert Howley and Austin Healey, but an injury to Howley and his good form for the mid-week side saw him make the starting line-up. He threw an outrageous dummy that fooled three South African defenders and then outpaced the cover to score a stunning solo try in the first Test.

The second Test was much tighter but Dawson fed Jeremy Guscott for the latter's

Above: *The 2003 England squad including Matt Dawson*

drop goal and the series was theirs. He had no time to bask in the glory of a series win over the world champions, however. He was selected as England captain on the notorious 'tour of hell' to the southern hemisphere the following year and presided over the heaviest defeat in the country's history (76-0 against Australia). His performances rarely warranted criticism, however, and he captained the side when Martin Johnson and Lawrence Dallaglio were unavailable.

He was again behind Rob Howley in the pecking order for the 2001 Lions tour to Australia but Howley was injured before the decisive third Test. Dawson stepped in but couldn't prevent Australia snatching a last-

gasp series win. The tour had hardly finished when Dawson published memoirs vehemently criticizing Graham Henry and his coaching staff.

Dawson won his 50th cap on the day England won the 2003 Grand Slam. It was a golden year for English rugby as they went on to defeat Australia and New Zealand in their own backyards on their way to clinching the Webb Ellis Trophy in Sydney in November (where Dawson made a crucial break before supplying Wilkinson with the final pass). He remains England's most-capped scrum-half (77 appearances – nine as captain), and, with his quick hands, unorthodox style, sniping runs around the scrum and tap-and-go penalties, he played an integral role in making England a real force at the beginning of the 21st century.

Having made a few appearances on the BBC's A Question of Sport, Dawson called time on his international career in 2005 after a disappointing Lions tour to New Zealand. He then made several appearances on Strictly Come Dancing and Celebrity Masterchef. He now enjoys a full-time media career.

Name: Matthew James Sutherland Dawson, MBE
Born: 31st October 1972, Birkenhead
Home Union: England
Position: Scrum-half
Height / Weight: 5'10" (1.78m) /
Lions Tours: South Africa (1997), Australia (2001), New Zealand (2005)
Number of Tests: 7
Points: 10

Dawson, Ronnie

Dawson qualified as an architect and played his club rugby with Wanderers FC from 1950. He was also a Leinster stalwart on the provincial stage, playing 28 times between 1958 and 1964. His international debut was also in 1958, in a match against Australia. Ireland won and he was promoted to captain for the next 11 games.

His strong leadership and quality at the set-piece and breakdown saw him selected as captain for the 1959 Lions. His six Tests in the role wasn't equalled until Martin Johnson led the team for all three Tests in South Africa in 1997 and Australia four years later. He was unavailable for the 1962 side but did return to duty with the Lions as assistant manager for the 1968 tour to South Africa, and he has also held a position on the selection committee.

He retired from international rugby in 1965 with 27 Ireland caps, six for the Lions and a reputation for developing new coaching techniques. He subsequently became a successful rugby administrator and was a dedicated Home Union Committee member for more than 20 years. He was rewarded for his service to the game in 2004 when he was presented with the IRB's Vernon Pugh Award.

Above: *Ronnie Dawson leads the Lions out against the All Blacks in 1959*

Name: Alfred Ronald 'Ronnie' Dawson
Born: 5th June 1932, Dublin
Home Union: Ireland
Position: Hooker
Height / Weight: 5'11" (1.80m) / 176lbs (80kg)
Lions Tours: Australia & New Zealand (1959), and as assistant manager: South Africa (1968)
Number of Tests: 6
Points: 3

Dooley

Known as 'The Blackpool Tower', Wade Dooley was an old–school lock who formed a formidable partnership with Paul Ackford in England's second row during one of the most successful periods in the national side's history. England had silky backs like Rory Underwood and Jeremy Guscott but if they were going to win titles they also needed rugged, uncompromising forwards and they didn't come much better than Dooley.

He played rugby league as a teenager but converted to union when he was 19. He declined to play his domestic rugby at the highest level and remained with the Preston Grasshoppers under the tutelage of former England coach Dick Greenwood, although his refusal to join a top–flight club may have been why he had to wait until he was 27 for his first cap (against Romania in 1985). He made up for lost time and was a regular in the team for the next eight years, a period that included two Grand Slams and a World Cup final, although they narrowly lost the latter to Australia.

Dooley also went on the 1989 Lions tour to Australia and played in the final two Tests of the series, both of which the Lions won. When he played his last game for England in 1993 he was his country's most–capped second row. His Lions career came to a premature end when he was the victim of a poor decision by the tour management, however. During the 1993 trip to New Zealand he flew home to be at his father's funeral but he was then replaced by Martin Johnson. No one had a problem with Johnson's inclusion on the tour – indeed the young Leicester lock would go on to become one of the finest players in the world – but the way the situation was handled was totally insensitive and his achievements deserved a more sympathetic approach. Dooley realised there was no way back and retired shortly afterwards.

Name: Wade Anthony Dooley
Born: 2nd October 1957, Warrington
Home Union: England
Position: Lock
Height / Weight: 6'8" (2.03m) / 252lbs (114kg)
Lions Tours: Australia (1989)
Number of Tests: 2
Points: 0

Duckham

Born in the Midlands and educated at a grammar school, Duckham quickly established himself in the Coventry side and developed into one of the best centres in the country. He had a blistering turn of pace, devastating sidestep and sublime handling and, when England were in one of their darkest periods in the mid-1970s, his pairing with John Spencer brought some hope to a beleaguered side. Indeed they were perhaps the only players who could live with the gloriously gifted Welsh and French three-quarters.

He made his debut for England against Ireland in 1969 and announced himself on the world stage with a spectacular 60-yard run and score. He was also one of the lynchpins in the side that beat South Africa later that season. He was then selected for the Lions tour to New Zealand two years later. Coach Carwyn James encouraged him to use his flair and he flourished alongside the great Welshmen. He scored 11 tries in 16 matches on the tour – including six in one match – and James selected him ahead of John Bevan for the final three Tests that saw the Lions clinch the series and return home triumphant.

When people recall rugby's most famous game – the Barbarians against New Zealand at the Arms Park in 1973 – it is easy to forget that Duckham was the only Englishman in the backline. During one move he fooled the commentator, cameraman and several Kiwi defenders with such an outrageous sidestep and break that it drew cheers from the Welsh crowd and earned him the nickname Dai.

Legendary television commentator Bill McLaren also ranked him up with the best, saying that even if you knew the famous sidestep was coming you could do little about it. There's no doubt that he would have scored even more tries had the England pack given the backs more ball but this was a lean period in English rugby history and he didn't get the service his talent deserved.

Duckham was awarded an MBE for services to rugby in 1977, and he also wrote an autobiography, Dai for England, acknowledging how he was known to the Welsh in the 1970s. He is also an honorary president of the Wooden Spoon Foundation that helps improve the lives of disadvantaged children.

Name: David John Duckham, MBE
Born: 28th June 1946, Coventry
Home Union: England
Position: Centre
Height / Weight: 6'1" (1.86m) / 205lbs (93kg)
Lions Tours: New Zealand (1971)
Number of Tests: 3
Points: 0

DUCKHAM

Duggan

Duggan was an old-school forward who played hard and partied hard. He was first capped by Ireland in 1975 and would go on to appear 41 times for his country and be

promoted to captain in 1984. His combative nature saw him become the first Irishman sent off during a Five Nations international (against Wales in 1977), although he didn't view the incident as seriously as those watching. "The referee politely asked me if I minded leaving the field, to which I replied 'No problem, I'm buggered anyway.'"

Duggan was selected for the 1977 Lions tour to New Zealand as he was one of the few forwards who enjoyed genuine respect from the Kiwi players. His training methods may have left a little to be desired – he once famously handed the referee his cigarette as he took the field – but there's no doubting his commitment, work ethic and ferociousness in the tackle.

The tour may not have been a huge success in terms of results, but Duggan remains one of the best-loved figures in Irish sporting history.

Left: Willie Duggan in action for the Lions

Name: William Patrick Duggan
Born: 12th March 1950
Home Union: Ireland
Position: Number 8
Height / Weight: 6'4" (1.93m) / 220lbs (100kg)
Lions Tours: New Zealand (1977)
Number of Tests: 4
Points: 4

Edwards

Right: *Gareth Edwards (left) and Phil Bennett*

Edwards was the son of a miner who was educated at Pontardawe Technical School. His sublime skills were spotted by sports teacher Bill Samuels who suggested he try for a sports scholarship to Millfield School in Somerset. He was an accomplished gymnast, athlete and footballer, and he signed for Swansea as a 16-year-old.

The lure of playing rugby for Wales at the beginning of their golden era in the late 1960s proved too much, however, and Edwards was handed his first cap in 1967 at the age of 20 against France in Paris. He was given the captaincy in 1968 and then played in a record 58 consecutive matches for his country, never suffering an injury or loss of form.

Edwards turned 21 on his first Lions tour to South Africa in 1968. His half-back partnership with Barry John was still in its infancy and the team were not good enough to trouble their hosts. However, in New Zealand three years later, the pairing were at their devastating best. As long as rugby is played, the argument will rage over which of the 1971 and 1974 sides was better but what is certain is that Edwards played the key role in both successes. He was the best scrum-half of the era – perhaps of any era – and his devastating breaks, elusive running and fine distribution edged the series for the Lions. Although he was forced off the field with a leg injury during the first Test, he returned

for the remainder of the series and produced his finest performance in the third match when his break opened the All Black defence down the blindside and he created a try for Gerald Davies.

In 1973 Edwards scored the greatest try in the history of the game when he finished off a move started by Phil Bennett in his own 25. It was a score of breathtaking beauty and it ensured the Barbarians beat the mighty All Blacks in Cardiff.

In South Africa a year later, Edwards was at his peak. His forwards destroyed the Springbok

pack and allowed him so much time and space that he could control the pace of the game single-handedly. He slotted the decisive drop goal in the first Test and delivered a pinpoint reverse pass for Phil Bennett to seal the series win with another drop. Willie John McBride promptly described him as the best scrum-half he had ever seen or was ever likely to see, high praise indeed from the legendary Lion. His outstanding contribution to the tour led to him being awarded the 1974 BBC Sports Personality of the Year.

He was equally impressive in the Five Nations, winning the championship seven times and recording three Grand Slams. He retired in 1978 and was immediately back in the spotlight when he became captain on A Question of Sport. In 1997 he was one of the first inductees into the Hall of Fame, and in 2001 he was voted the greatest Welsh player of all time. It's unusual

to finish a piece on Edwards with a contribution from an Englishman but former England captain Will Carling summed up his impact on the game thus: "Edwards was a supreme athlete with supreme skills. His running, passing, kicking and reading of the game were outstanding and he sits astride the whole of planet rugby."

In 2003 Rugby World magazine voted him the greatest player of all time.

Name: Gareth Owen Edwards, CBE
Born: 12th July 1947, Pontardawe
Home Union: Wales
Position: Scrum-half
Height / Weight: 5'8" (1.73m) / 165lbs (75kg)
Lions Tours: South Africa (1968), New Zealand (1971), South Africa (1974)
Number of Tests: 10
Points: 3

Evans

Evans's rugby career began at the Queen Elizabeth Grammar School and then Carmarthen Quins. He joined Llanelli at the age of 19 and eventually played in seven cup finals for the team, of which they won five. He then joined Bath and helped the side to the 1998 European Cup.

His international career was equally glittering. He made his debut for Wales in Paris in 1987 and immediately proved himself a winger with great speed and skill. He was selected for the Lions to Australia in 1989 and scored the decisive try in the third Test after a mistake by David Campese. He also scored a magnificent try against England at the Arms Park in 1993 and captained Wales to the Five Nations Championship the following year.

His second Lions tour showed he was still at the peak of his powers and his four tries saw him as the tourists' top scorer. He couldn't help them to a series win, however, but he was back with the team in South Africa four years later. Although more of a fringe player towards the end of his career, he still helped the Lions to victory over the world champions.

Evans retired at the end of the following season but his record stands up against the best in the game. Seventy-two caps for his country – of which 28 were as captain – and 33 tries puts him third on the Welsh all-time list behind only Shane Williams and Gareth Thomas.

He was awarded the MBE for services to the sport in 1996, and in 2007 he was inducted into the International Rugby Hall of Fame. He now works as a pundit for Sky TV's The Rugby Club and runs his own PR company.

Name: Ieuan Evans, MBE
Born: 21st March 1964, Pontardulais
Home Union: Wales
Position: Wing
Height / Weight: 5'10" (1.78m) / 187lbs (85kg)
Lions Tours: Australia (1989), New Zealand (1993), South Africa (1997)
Number of Tests: 7
Points: 5

Gibbs

Scott Gibbs will perhaps unfairly be remembered for two magic moments, the first a crunching hit on South African prop Os du Randt in the second Test of the 1997 Lions tour in Durban, and the second a jinking run to silence England in the last ever Five Nations match at Wembley in 1999. But Gibbs was much more than a two-hit wonder.

The slight centre started his career at Pencoed RFC and he soon graduated to senior rugby with Bridgend. He was capped by his country in 1991 but he needed a higher class of club rugby if his career was going to progress. He joined Swansea and had an immediate impact, helping himself to a hatful of tries and the club to the 1992 cup final at the Arms Park (they eventually lost to Llanelli).

Despite being only 22 he was selected for the 1993 Lions tour to New Zealand and he raised a few eyebrows by being picked for the team in the second and third Tests ahead of England captain Will Carling. He justified his place in the team, however, and was one of the stars of the tour.

There was criticism over his size though, so he spent a number of years bulking up with rugby league side St Helens. As the union code then went professional, Gibbs flitted between the two, playing for Wales at the 1995 World Cup and then helping St Helens to the Challenge Cup and Super League titles the following year.

The 1997 Lions tour to South Africa was a success on every level and Gibbs's bullocking run and huge hit on du Randt lifted the entire squad and gave them much-needed momentum. He was later voted 'player of the series'.

His Wembley try two years later sank England by a point, denying them the last Five Nations Championship and handing the title to Scotland. He was again selected for Lions duty on the 2001 tour to Australia but by then he was past his best and he didn't play in the Test team. He retired from international duty with 53 caps and he occasionally returns to our screens with the BBC. He now lives in South Africa.

Above: Scott Gibbs in action

Name: Ian Scott Gibbs
Born: 23rd January 1971, Bridgend
Home Union: Wales
Position: Centre
Height / Weight: 5'9" (1.75m) / 217lbs (98kg)
Lions Tours: New Zealand (1993), South Africa (1997), Australia (2001)
Number of Tests: 5
Points: 5

Gibson

Former Cambridge University three-quarter Mike Gibson was a rugby perfectionist, but he was good enough to meet the standards he set for himself. He was perhaps the greatest centre in the game's history and his longevity – five Lions tours – proves he could always mix it with the best from the southern hemisphere.

His brilliance lay in the perception and timing of his runs, the anticipation and power of his defence, and the commitment to stay at the top for 15 years and a then-record 81 international appearances.

His first two tours gave him valuable experience, and he became the first replacement in top-flight rugby when he came on in the opening Test against South Africa in 1968. With Barry John out injured, Gibson played in 11 of the next 13 matches and didn't disappoint. His finest hour came on the New Zealand tour in 1971, when he teamed up with John and John Dawes to form arguably the perfect midfield trio.

The host crowds loved his blistering runs and perfectly timed passing. In the second Test it was Gibson's beautiful interplay with JPR Williams and Gerald Davies that sent the latter flying up the wing to score having destroyed the world's best defence in the blink of an eye.

Gibson joined the 1974 tour as a replacement and he displayed a remarkable lack of ego in willingly playing understudy – and passing on his wisdom – to the new Test pairing of Ian McGeechan and Dick Milliken. He equalled Willie John McBride's record of five Lions tours in 1977 but injuries prevented him from competing for a Test place. It was a tame end to a brilliant career, although the All Blacks must have been delighted to see the back of him.

Name: Cameron Michael Henderson 'Mike' Gibson, MBE
Born: 3rd December 1942, Belfast
Home Union: Ireland
Position: Centre
Height / Weight: 5'11" (1.80m) / 178lbs (81kg)
Lions Tours: Australia & New Zealand (1966), South Africa (1968), New Zealand (1971), South Africa (1974), New Zealand (1977)
Number of Tests: 12
Points: 0

Greenwood, Jim

Greenwood played for Dunfermline RFC and was called up by Scotland for their Five Nations encounter with France in 1952. He had a torrid first game and was dropped for the next two years, although when he came back it was as captain. He was a solid and mobile back-row forward who had quick hands and a good turn of pace. He was also strong in the tackle. This overall dependability saw him captain his country for three years, as well as earning him a spot on the 1955 Lions tour to South Africa.

He played in all four Tests on the trip and helped the side to two wins and a share of the series. He was an advocate for the 15-man rugby that would become prevalent in the 1960s and '70s and was a firm believer that the better teams encouraged players to play in every position. The tour was a great success, with the Lions winning 19 of 25 matches.

When Greenwood retired he returned to teaching at Glenalmond College. He died aged 81 in 2010.

Left: *Jim Greenwood*

> **Name:** James Thomson 'Jim' Greenwood
> **Born:** 2nd December 1928, Dunfermline
> **Died:** 13th September 2010, Dumfries
> **Home Union:** Scotland
> **Position:** Number 8, Flanker
> **Height / Weight:** 6'2" (1.88m) / 196lbs (89kg)
> **Lions Tours:** South Africa (1955)
> **Number of Tests:** 4
> **Points:** 0

Greenwood, Will

Right: *Will Greenwood of England breaks through the tackle of Scott Murray of Scotland*

The son of former England player and coach Dick Greenwood, Will was educated at Stonyhurst College and then Sedbergh School. He initially worked in the City but a career in rugby was the aim and he joined Leicester from Harlequins. He then became part of the England set-up under Clive Woodward in 1997. Until then, Will Carling had been the captain so there was no chance of him playing. He also played for Preston Grasshoppers and Waterloo, before returning to 'Quins in 2000. He made his England debut against Australia and the All Blacks in 1997, and quickly developed a rapport with fellow centres Jeremy Guscott and Mike Tindall. When Jonny Wilkinson joined the fray, the pieces were all in place for England to mount an assault on the World Cup. There were domestic obstacles to overcome first, however.

Greenwood was overlooked for the 1997 Six Nations, but he was selected for that year's Lions tour to South Africa as the squad's only uncapped player. Injury prevented him from making a Test appearance, however. (For superstitious reasons he always wore the No 13 jersey but he wasn't given the shirt on the tour and was knocked unconscious.) He was also unlucky in 2001, losing out to Brian O'Driscoll and Rob Henderson, but he finally made his Lions debut in 2005 when O'Driscoll was injured by the Umaga / Mealamu spear tackle just minutes into the first Test.

Two year earlier, Greenwood had been one of England's best players when they won the Grand Slam and then beat Australia and New Zealand in their own backyards. He was also an integral part of the World Cup-winning team. He played in six of the seven matches, was involved in all of England's tries bar Jason Robinson's in the final, and finished joint top scorer with five. None of these scores was more important than the charge down against a powerful South Africa side that gave England a handy cushion, and finishing off Jason's Robinson's blistering counterattack against Wales when they looked like they were heading for defeat. His defence in the final was exceptional, as was his celebration at the final whistle.

He was England's top try scorer in both the 2002 and 2003 Six Nations Championships, and he reached more milestones in the 2004 tournament: appointed England vice-captain

under Lawrence Dallaglio, then earning his 50th cap against Ireland.

He won the last of his 55 England caps against Australia in 2004, and reluctantly retired two years later after a sterling career for both club and country. As England slipped down the world rankings in 2005 and 2006, Greenwood was one of the players England missed the most. The side seemed bereft of options without his deft passing, eye for a gap, solid defence and ability to read the game. He was awarded the MBE in 2003.

He scored 31 tries for England (only Rory Underwood, with 49, has more), and he also brought this killer instinct to his club rugby. His match-winning score against Brive in the quarter-final of the 2001 European Shield was voted try of the season. They lost a dramatic

Pilkington Cup final to Newcastle Falcons, although a winners' medal with Leicester Tigers in 1997 was some consolation. He is now an analyst for Sky Sports and writes for The Daily Telegraph.

Name: William John Heaton 'Will' Greenwood, MBE
Born: 20th October 1972, Blackburn, Lancashire
Home Union: England
Position: Centre
Height / Weight: 6'4" (1.93m) / 220lbs (100kg)
Lions Tours: South Africa (1997), Australia (2001), New Zealand (2005)
Number of Tests: 2
Points: 0

Guscott

Right: Jeremy Guscott clears the ball

Guscott supported local side Bath from a young age, and he had soon joined their youth team. He made his debut for the senior club as a teenager in 1984 and his turn of pace, silky skills and solid defence saw him called up for the national team against Romania in 1989. He announced himself on the international stage by scoring a hat-trick. This was the amateur era, however, and Guscott held down various jobs – labourer, PR man, model – to make ends meet.

His centre partnership with Will Carling ushered in England's most successful period to date. They narrowly missed out on a Grand Slam in 1990 but made sure in 1991 (a year they also made the World Cup final), 1992 and 1995. The World Cup in South Africa brought it home to England that, although they may be dominant in the northern hemisphere, they were well behind the All Blacks in terms of professionalism, fitness, preparation and tactics. Guscott was one of the few who adapted to the modern era, earning his 'prince of centres' nickname with his line breaks and sublime handling. His international career came to a premature end after he sustained a groin injury during the 1999 World Cup but, at the time, his record of 30 tries in 65 appearances was only bettered by Rory Underwood. He retired a year later.

As a Lion, Guscott will go down in history for his drop goal that secured the 1997 series at the end of the second Test against South Africa. He'd already toured with the victorious 1989 party to Australia, although he was less successful four years later in New Zealand. Domestically he was part of a Bath team that ruled the roost in England, and in 1998 he helped Bath become the first English team to lift the European Cup.

Guscott is now a regular panellist for the BBC.

Name: Jeremy Clayton Guscott, MBE
Born: 7th July 1965, Bath
Home Union: England
Position: Centre
Height / Weight: 6'1" (1.85m) / 185lbs (84kg)
Lions Tours: Australia (1989), New Zealand (1993), South Africa (1997)
Number of Tests: 8
Points: 7

Hastings

The list of Scottish full-backs who have played for the Lions is both long and illustrious, from Dan Drysdale and Charlie Grieve in 1924 and 1938 to Angus Cameron, Ken Scotland, Stewart Wilson and Andy Irvine. Gavin Hastings was arguably the finest of them all, however.

Whereas Irvine was the more complete footballer – with his counterattacking style he played more like a wing – Hastings was more conventional: solid beneath the high ball, powerful coming into the line, physically strong in the tackle, accurate kicking from the hand off both feet, and superb in front of goal. The model London Scottish and Watsonians full-back was therefore a key figure on two Lions tours and he captained the side in New Zealand in 1993.

Four years earlier Gavin and brother Scott made history in Australia by becoming the first brothers to appear in the same Lions team. There's no doubt that their understanding in the midfield played a pivotal role in the crucial match of the series. Gavin collected Scott's pass, sold a dummy and handed off David Campese to score. Hastings had been concussed early in the half and only realised he'd scored when he watched a replay after the match. The Lions won the Test and levelled the series.

Four years later, his good form with Scotland earned him the Lions captaincy ahead of Will Carling. The Lions lost the series against the All Blacks but Hastings kicked all of the Lions' points in the first Test only to see them lose 20-18 after a controversial last-minute penalty. Despite suffering with a pulled hamstring, he struck another 12 points in the second Test and the tourists recorded their biggest win over New Zealand. Sadly they couldn't raise themselves for the decisive Test and were soundly beaten.

He remains the second highest scorer in Lions history with 66 points (Jonny Wilkinson has 67), second on the all-time list for Scotland with 667 (Chris Paterson has 809), and second in rugby World Cups with 227 (Wilkinson has 277). He is widely considered as the best Scottish player of all time and one of the best full-backs the game has seen.

Name: Andrew Gavin Hastings, OBE
Born: 3rd January 1962, Edinburgh
Home Union: Scotland
Position: Full-back
Height / Weight: 6'2" (1.88m) / 199lbs (91kg)
Lions Tours: Australia (1989), New Zealand (1993)
Number of Tests: 6
Points: 66

Hewitt

HEWITT

Right: *David Hewitt poses for a publicity shot*

Hewitt was an extremely talented centre who never quite fulfilled his potential. For the Lions, though, his blistering runs, accurate kicking and pinpoint passes helped the wings outside him score almost at will. Hewitt came from a sporting family – his father, two uncles and two cousins all played for Ireland – and he made his debut against Australia at Landsdowne Road at the back end of 1958. By the end of the season, he was a Lion.

The Belfast law student was the quickest man in the squad but he also had speed of thought that gave him time to make the right decisions in attack and defence. A back injury ruled him out of the second Test in New Zealand but he still made 18 appearances on the tour and scored 112 points, including 13 tries. In the third Test he made a searing break and beat two defenders with a deft weave off his left foot before touching down for the try of the match. He was criticised for delaying a crucial pass that would have given Tony O'Reilly a try later in the game but it didn't take the gloss off a tremendous individual performance.

Three years later, he was selected for the Lions tour to South Africa, but he was restricted to just seven starts by hamstring injuries that would then plague him for the rest of his career. He retired from the game in 1965 after Ireland's Five Nations visit to Cardiff Arms Park.

Name: David Hewitt
Born: 9th September 1939, Belfast
Home Union: Ireland
Position: Centre
Height / Weight: 5'9" (1.76m) / 169lbs (77kg)
Lions Tours: Australia & New Zealand (1959), South Africa (1962)
Number of Tests: 6
Points: 16

Hill

Often referred to as the 'silent assassin' for his quiet but abrasive style, Hill joined the England fold in 1997 having done his apprenticeship at Saracens. He came on against Scotland as open-side flanker ahead of Neil Back, but Clive Woodward was happy to reorganise the pack to accommodate Hill and he switched him to blindside flanker. From then on, Hill was never dropped by Woodward. Other players came and went but Hill's form never dipped and there was real concern that an injury picked up in the opening game of the 2003 World Cup would hamper his side's chances of winning. Fortunately the triumvirate of Back, Dallaglio and Hill was available for the final.

Hill was equally effective in attack and defence and he scored 12 tries in his 71 internationals. He was consistently England's top tackler and was always doing the hard graft at the coalface while lesser mortals wilted. He made the first of three successive Lions squads in 1997 and earned two caps on the tour of South Africa. He failed to finish either of the 2001 or 2005 tours to Australia and New Zealand, however. He was deliberately and shamefully taken out by a stray elbow by Nathan Grey in the second Test in Australia when the tourists were clearly on top. The resulting concussion saw him sidelined for the remainder of the tour, and it was doubtless a turning point in the series.

The Lions missed his work-rate and offensive power terribly and they narrowly lost a Test they probably would have won had he been fit.

He then injured his knee early on the 2005 trip to New Zealand – not even a player of Hill's class could have salvaged anything from a disappointing series – and the rugby world was denied the most eagerly anticipated contest of the series: his potential head-to-head with Kiwi skipper Richie McCaw.

He retired from international rugby in 2008 as one of the most respected and well-liked flankers in the game's history.

Name: Richard Anthony Hill, MBE
Born: 23rd May 1973
Home Union: England
Position: Flanker
Height / Weight: 6'2" (1.88m) / 238lbs (108kg)
Lions Tours: South Africa (1997), Australia (2001), New Zealand (2005)
Number of Tests: 5
Points: 0

Howley

Right: Rob Howley is now head coach of Wales

Howley played for local side Bridgend before joining Cardiff. He made his Wales debut in 1996 and made such an impact that he was then selected for the 1997 Lions tour to South Africa. His personal duel with Springbok legend Joost van der Westhuizen was one of the most eagerly anticipated match-ups of the series but Howley picked up a shoulder injury and was ruled out of the Tests. It was a bitter blow for a player who was fast-becoming the standout scrum-half in world rugby.

Howley helped Wales defeat England at Wembley in the last Five Nations encounter in 1999 and he was on such good form for the next two seasons that he was again picked for the Lions on their 2001 tour to Australia. Howley played in the first two Tests but then picked up another injury and he missed the decisive third Test, which the tourists lost.

He moved from Cardiff to London Wasps but more injuries curtailed his career and he announced his retirement in 2004. Had it not been for bad luck and this spate of injuries, Howley would now be remembered as one of the game's great number nines. As it is, two Lions tours, 59 caps for his country, of which 22 were as captain, and ten Test tries still see him ranked by his peers as a scrum-half of real talent.

He worked with the Wales squad as an assistant coach in the build-up to the 2013 Six Nations Championship but took over the head coach's role before their opening fixture against Ireland. He will also travel to Australia with the Lions.

> **Name:** Robert Howley
> **Born:** 13th October 1970, Bridgend
> **Home Union:** Wales
> **Position:** Scrum-half
> **Height / Weight:** 5'9" (1.75m) / 187lbs (85kg)
> **Lions Tours:** South Africa (1997, Australia (2001), and as assistant coach: Australia (2013)
> **Number of Tests:** 2
> **Points:** 0

Irvine

Andy Irvine is sometimes unfairly remembered primarily as a goal-kicker, and indeed his reliability in front of the posts earned him club, country, Lions and world points-scoring records, but it was his flair with the ball in hand for which he should be celebrated.

He wasn't good enough to displace JPR Williams at full-back so his Lions Test career began on the wing. He came into the 1974 side for two Tests instead of Billy Steele after the latter's fitness and form had dipped. Irvine still chipped in with a record 156 points on the tour, however. Three years later, he'd developed his attacking game and was the danger man in the back division. He displayed his full repertoire of jinking runs and defence-splitting passing against the New Zealand defences, and he racked up 25 points in a single match against Hanan Shield. He then scored five tries in the game against King Country-Wanganui.

He carried a tweaked hamstring into the 1980 series in South Africa but he was forced to play when other members of the tour picked up more serious injuries. He made eight appearances in all and played in the final three Tests. He capped his Lions career with one of the tries that won the final match and promptly retired as international rugby's leading points-scorer.

He went on to coach Heriot's RFC before being appointed as president of the Scottish Rugby Union in 2005. Two years later he was appointed to the Lions selection committee and he was then asked to manage the 2013 tour to Australia. Few people could boast a better CV for the role.

Name: Andrew Robertson 'Andy' Irvine, MBE
Born: 16th September 1951, Edinburgh
Home Union: Scotland
Position: Full-back
Height / Weight: 5'10" (1.78m) / 176lbs (80kg)
Lions Tours: South Africa (1974), New Zealand (1977), South Africa (1980)
Number of Tests: 9
Points: 28

Jackson

Jackson was educated at King Edward VI School. He was invited to his first England trial while still at the Old Edwardians but made his name with Coventry – he would later become president of the club – and the 1951 Midlands XV that took on the South African tourists. Jackson also played for the army during his national service, was captain of Warwickshire and won the County Championship seven times in eight seasons between 1958 and 1965.

Like many great players of the post-war generation, however, Jackson – or Nijinsky as he was known to English fans – is remembered for one try in particular. It came at Twickenham in 1958 against the touring Australians. Late in the game, with the scores tied at 6-6 and England down to 14 men due to injury, Jackson gathered the ball more than 60 yards from the Australian line. He danced out of one tackle, sidestepped another and charged down the touchline. With only the full-back to beat, Jackson feinted inside, saw his man buy the dummy, and dived over in the corner to seal a historic win.

A year earlier Jackson had been one of the cornerstones of England's 1957 Grand Slam-winning team, a side that would eventually claim three Five Nations Championships. Jackson may have been a legend in Europe but he wasn't well known in the southern hemisphere until he visited New Zealand with the 1959 Lions side.

Jackson scored 19 tries on the tour, a tally only bettered by Ireland's Tony O'Reilly, and earned his second nickname, Pimpernel, because the Kiwi defences simply couldn't get near him. His try sealed the Lions' win in the fourth Test (9-6) but his form suffered when he returned home and he didn't play again until 1963. Indeed, most contemporary experts put England's poor 1961-62 season down to his absence.

Jackson died aged 73 in 2004 after a long illness.

Name: Peter Barrie Jackson
Born: 22nd September 1930, Birmingham
Died: 22nd March 2004, Solihull
Home Union: England
Position: Wing
Height / Weight: 5'11" (1.80m) / 169lbs (77kg)
Lions Tours: New Zealand (1959)
Number of Tests: 5
Points: 6

Jeeps

Dickie Jeeps was an outstanding all-rounder at school. He played cricket for his county, football for Cambridge and even dabbled in speed skating. He then developed into one of the greatest scrum-halves of his generation, but he earned his reputation as a Lion before establishing himself in the England team. Jeeps was an influential pivot behind Northampton's scrum but didn't get the opportunity to prove himself on the world stage until he was selected for Peter Jackson's 1955 Lions in South Africa. Cliff Morgan had played against Jeeps and recommended him to the selectors, and they duly called him up.

He set a post-war record by being only the second Englishman to play a game of Test rugby for the Lions before representing his home union. Jeeps eventually toured three times with the Lions and played in 13 Tests, a record for an Englishman. Now that the tours are limited to three Tests, this record is unlikely to be beaten. He enjoyed an excellent tour and was immediately selected for England against Wales in 1956. Jeeps was made England captain for the 1959-60 Five Nations but the side narrowly missed out on a Grand Slam when they drew 3-3 with France. He proved himself once more with the Lions in New Zealand and was rewarded with the England captaincy for the next three years. He went on his last Lions tour back to South Africa in 1962.

With his playing days behind him, Jeeps became the RFU's youngest president at the age of 44 in 1975.

Name: Richard Eric Gautrey 'Dickie' Jeeps
Born: 25th November 1931, Chesterton
Home Union: England
Position: Scrum-half
Height / Weight: 5'7" (1.71m) / 167lbs (76kg)
Lions Tours: South Africa (1955), Australia & New Zealand (1959), South Africa (1962)
Number of Tests: 13
Points: 0

Jenkins

Right: *Neil Jenkins of Wales kicks a penalty*

Jenkins was a schoolboy player of some talent but it wasn't until a move to Ponypridd in 1990 that he became known to a wider audience. Good performances at fly-half and full-back saw him selected for Wales the following season, although the side was comprehensively outplayed by England in Cardiff and Jenkins missed out on selection for the World Cup squad.

Despite coming in for severe criticism over his perceived lack of pace and his preference for kicking, Jenkins worked on his all-round game and was soon the best distributor of flat passes to the backline that repeatedly opened up defences. His goal-kicking was second to none and he was his country's record points scorer before making his 30th start.

He was selected as a utility player for the 1997 Lions in South Africa but immediately proved his worth by keeping the scoreboard ticking over and pegging the Springboks back in their own half with his precise kicking from hand. The tourists secured the series win, and Jenkins was on hand again for his country when he notched the crucial conversion to beat England at Wembley.

In 2001 Jenkins became the first man to score 1,000 international points, and later that year he was selected for the Lions tour to Australia. He played second fiddle to Jonny Wilkinson but did come on late in the second Test. He was omitted from Wales's 2003 World Cup squad and retired from the game.

His 44 consecutive goal-kicks remains a world record, and his 1,090 international points sees him third on the all-time list behind Dan Carter and Wilkinson. He is now a member of the coaching staff for the national team.

Name: Neil Roger Jenkins, MBE
Born: 8th July 1971, Church Village
Home Union: Wales
Position: Full-back
Height / Weight: 5'10" (1.78m) / 190lbs (86kg)
Lions Tours: South Africa (1997), Australia (2001), and as kicking coach: South Africa (2009)
Number of Tests: 4
Points: 41

John, Barry

Above: *Barry John kicks the 1971 Lions to victory in New Zealand*

The supremely talented but diminutive Welshman was rugby's George Best, the game's first superstar. He didn't have the size to intimidate opponents but he made up for his physical shortcomings with a sensational sidestep off both feet, precise kicking and crisp passing. With Gareth Edwards inside him, this was perhaps the finest midfield pairing in the game's history.

John was lucky to be schooled in the sport's finer points by William Jones and Ray Williams, and it was while at grammar school that he made his first appearance for Llanelli in a match against Moseley. He was first capped by Wales in 1966 but his international career started slowly and he had to wait until the 1968 Lions tour before he emerged on the world stage.

The eagerly awaited battle with the Springboks' back row on John's first Lions tour ended 15 minutes into the first Test, however. John made a darting break for the line but was hauled down by Ellis and broke his collarbone on the hard ground.

The rugby world had to wait three more years before Edwards and John were once again pitted against the best from the southern hemisphere.

The pair guided the Lions to their only series win over the All Blacks. Their self-confidence bordered on arrogance but this infectious enthusiasm permeated the entire squad and they ripped the provincial sides to shreds. John masterminded the 47-9 annihilation of champions Wellington and scored a try of such beauty against a collective university side that the crowd was completely silenced. He finished the tour with 30 of the Lions' 48 Test points.

Then, while at the peak of his powers, he decided to retire at the age of just 27. The weight of expectation for club and country was proving too much and he felt like he was living in a goldfish bowl. The rugby world was therefore denied this mercurial talent, although his magical individual performances, goal-kicking records and peerless displays with both Wales and the Lions have cemented his god-like status to everyone who saw him play.

Not for nothing was Barry John known as 'The King'.

Name: Barry John
Born: 6th January 1945, Cefneithin
Home Union: Wales
Position: Fly-half
Height / Weight: 5'10" (1.78m) / 165lbs / 75kg
Lions Tours: South Africa (1968), New Zealand (1971)
Number of Tests: 5
Points: 30

Left:

John, Roy

John represented his local grammar school at rugby and showed such agility, pace and a deft sidestep for a big man that he joined Neath in his late teens. He made his international debut against England in the 1950 Five Nations but the team was expected to perform poorly as a number of new caps had been added to bolster a weak squad.

They beat England and then swept the other nations aside to complete a historic Grand Slam. He was selected for the 1950 Lions tour on the back of this and, together with club-mate Rees Stephens, they toiled away in the engine room for 22 tour matches, including all six Tests. They won two against Australia but only one of the four against New Zealand.

He was a regular in the Welsh squad for the next three Five Nations campaigns and only retired after 19 consecutive appearances in 1954. His finest moment came in his penultimate international, however, when Wales scored a rare victory over the touring All Blacks.

Name: Ernest Raymond 'Roy' John
Born: 3rd December 1925, Crynant
Died: 30th September 1981, Neath
Home Union: Wales
Position: Lock, Number 8
Height / Weight: 6'2" (1.88m) / 191lbs (87kg)
Lions Tours: Australia & New Zealand (1950)
Number of Tests: 6
Points: 3

Johnson

W hen the history of English rugby is written, Martin Johnson's name will be indelibly linked with it. He is rated by most experts as the greatest English player. The Leicester Tiger won every domestic and European honour in the game and on 22nd November 2003 he lifted the Webb Ellis trophy when England became the first northern hemisphere side to win the World Cup. Jonny Wilkinson's drop goal may have sealed the win against Australia but it was Johnson at the helm who masterminded the victory.

Johnson spent his late teens playing club rugby in New Zealand and he announced himself on the world stage when he deputised for Wade Dooley on the 1993 Lions tour. It was baptism of fire for the young lock but his reputation grew over the next four years and he was chosen to lead the tourists in South Africa in 1997. Under coaches Ian McGeechan and Jim Telfer, Johnson led the side to a 2-1 series win against the world champions.

Four years later, he was again chosen as captain for the tour to Australia. Former Ireland captain Keith Wood played alongside Johnson on both tours and rated him as the best captain he'd ever had, a man who let his actions do his talking. Johnson was a master at disrupting the opposition's game, turning over their ball and driving them back in the tackle. He played on the edge and pushed referees to the limit.

Left: *Martin Johnson of England takes the ball in the lineout*

As captain of Leicester, Johnson was named Allied Dunbar Premiership Player of the Season in 1999 and he guided them through the most successful period in the club's history. He led the club to four successive Premiership titles (1999-2002), two domestic cups, and back-to-back Heineken Cups (2001 and 2002). It was no surprise that they went three seasons without a trophy after his retirement in 2005.

He was the central figure and outstanding player on the international stage in the same period, overseeing remarkable wins over the southern hemisphere giants at Twickenham and on their own patches. England's Grand Slam in early 2003 hinted at what was to come and he also steered the side to famous wins in Australia (now known as the 'massacre in Melbourne') and New

Zealand during the build-up to the World Cup. When England's pack was reduced to six men in Wellington (Lawrence Dallaglio and Neil Back were both sin-binned), Johnson took the game by the scruff of the neck and kept the All Blacks at bay almost single-handedly. He retired from international rugby after the tournament and it was no coincidence that England then endured four years in the wilderness.

Johnson was made CBE in the 2004 New Year honours. He couldn't stay out of the limelight for long and returned to coach the national team when Brian Ashton stepped down in 2008. But this was a difficult period for English rugby and the team was still in transition after their heroics at the 2007 World Cup. By 2011, however, the team had started to perform and, despite a Grand Slam-denying loss to Ireland, the side won the Six Nations and were expected to do well at the World Cup in New Zealand. It proved a false dawn, however. England performed poorly on and off the pitch and Johnson stepped down.

Name: Martin Osborne Johnson, CBE
Born: 9th March 1970, Solihull, West Midlands
Home Union: England
Position: Lock
Height / Weight: 6'7" (2.01m) / 261lbs (119kg)
Lions Tours: New Zealand (1993), South Africa (1997), Australia (2001)
Number of Tests: 8
Points: 0

Jones, Lewis

L ewis Jones first played rugby at grammar school and he then joined Neath. After

serving in the navy he moved to Llanelli and was called up for Wales in their 1950 Five Nations match with England. He was then asked to join the Lions after injury had ruled out several players from the Test side.

He made an immediate impact, scoring 63 points in his seven matches in New Zealand and another 16 against Australia in Brisbane. Realising he could cash in on his ability and fame, Jones signed for Leeds rugby league in 1952. He didn't take long to settle in and scored 302 points in only his second season.

He played for Great Britain 15 times and scored in every match. He is one of the few players to be honoured by both codes and remains one of the finest exponents in the games' history.

Name: Benjamin Lewis Jones
Born: 11th April 1931, Swansea
Home Union: Wales
Position: Full–back, centre, wing
Lions Tours: Australia & New Zealand (1950)
Number of Tests: 3
Points: 26

Jones, Ken

Jones was a student at West Monmouth Grammar School and he soon developed into a rugby player of considerable skill and blistering pace. He concentrated on his sprinting while serving in the army during the war and he was selected for the sprint relay team at the 1948 Olympic Games in London. He collected a silver medal and then joined Newport RFC.

By now he was a regular in the Welsh national side and he was soon running in tries from all parts of the field. In 1950 his scores ensured that they won their first Grand Slam since 1911. He didn't always get the service his class merited when playing for club or country but that changed on the 1950 Lions tour to Australia and New Zealand. He ran in 17 tries in 17 matches and played in three of the four Tests against the Kiwis. He scored a magnificent solo try in the fourth Test and was about to touchdown for the winner when the ball bounced awkwardly and eluded him.

He retired from international rugby in 1957 with 44 caps and 51 points under his belt. He was the inaugural winner of the Welsh Sports Personality of the Year and picked up an OBE in 1960. He was also the first rugby union inductee into the Welsh Sports Hall of Fame.

He died at the age of 85 in 2006.

Name: Kenneth Jeffrey 'Ken' Jones, OBE
Born: 30th December 1921, Blaenavon
Died: 18th April 2006, Newport
Home Union: Wales
Position: Wing
Height / Weight: 5'11" (1.80m) / 172lbs (78kg)
Lions Tours: Australia & New Zealand (1950)
Number of Tests: 3
Points: 3

Jones, Robert

Robert Jones made his debut for Swansea as a teenager and he was soon being mentioned in the same breath as the Welsh greats of the past. He formed a formidable half-back partnership with Jonathan Davies before the stand-off switched codes and joined rugby league outfit Widnes, although they both played an important part in Wales's 1988 Triple Crown. In the match against Scotland, Jones flung an enormous reverse pass to Davies, with the latter then chipping through to score. He also supplied the key passes for Davies's two drop goals that sealed the match.

Jones was promptly chosen to tour Australia with the Lions, during which he arguably got the better of Wallaby legend Nick Farr-Jones. The Lions secured a 2-1 series win and Jones was ever-present for Wales in the next Five Nations on the back of his performances. He toured again with the Lions to New Zealand in 1993 – in what would be the last amateur series – but he didn't play a major role and couldn't help the team overcome the mighty All Blacks in the Tests.

Jones retired from international rugby in 1995 having played 54 times for Wales and three times for the Lions. He was an accomplished and technical scrum-half with a killer pass, deft hands and a quick turn of pace around the ruck. He hung up his boots in 2001 but he can still be heard commentating on BBC radio and works as an assistant coach at Llanelli.

Above: *Robert Jones of the British Lions passes the ball*

Name: Robert Nicholas Jones
Born: 10th November 1965, Trebanos
Home Union: Wales
Position: Scrum-half
Height / Weight: 5'8" (1.73m) / 162lbs (73kg)
Lions Tours: Australia (1989). New Zealand (1993)
Number of Tests: 3
Points: 0

Kiernan

Right: *Irish rugby player Tom Kiernan.*

Kiernan was an exceptional player in his youth and he was tipped for greatness from an early age. He didn't disappoint and went on to become one of the game's great full-backs. He joined Munster and was fast-tracked into the Ireland side at the age of only 21. By the time he retired in 1973 he'd racked up the most Test appearances by an Irishman (54), most Tests as captain (22), most points (158) and two tours with the Lions.

It's unusual for a full-back to captain a side but Kiernan was so influential for Ireland that, having already toured with the Lions twice, he was chosen to lead the 1968 tourists to South Africa. He had only played once for the team before but on this trip he played in all four internationals, although the series was eventually lost 3-0, the same result as back in 1962. The midweek side enjoyed great success, however, winning 15 of their 16 matches and only losing to Transvaal.

Five years after his international retirement he coached Munster to perhaps their greatest win when they defeated the All Blacks, the first time any Irish team had beaten the Kiwis in more than a century.

Name: Thomas Joseph Kiernan
Born: 7th January 1939, Cork
Home Union: Ireland
Position: Full-back
Height / Weight: 5'10" (1.78m) / 161lbs (73kg)
Lions Tours: South Africa (1962), Australia & New Zealand (1966), South Africa (1968)
Number of Tests: 5
Points: 35

Kyle

Jack Kyle has been voted Ireland's best player, and there are some in New Zealand and Australia who rate him the greatest Lion. The Belfast-born fly-half was lightning-quick over short distances, delivered precise passes and could step off both feet and leave defenders clutching thin air. He was also a fine kicker and a better tackler than most people gave him credit for.

This combination of speed and skill helped Ireland to their only Grand Slam to date in 1948 but it was on the 1950 Lions tour to New Zealand that he earned his spurs. Still only 24, he was a sufficiently rounded talent to be named in New Zealand Rugby Almanac's players of the year.

With the likes of Jack Matthews and Bleddyn Williams in the centre, he could always play on the gain line and his passing gave these devastating runners the time and space they needed to scythe through the All Black defence. His best game came in the first Test in which he scored a spectacular solo try having counterattacked from a miscued kick. He sliced through the Kiwi rearguard, then set up another try for Jones with a pinpoint kick, and also won the penalty that almost gave them the game. The Lions could only draw 9-9, however, and the series slipped away when they narrowly lost the next three Tests.

He scored another try in the 24-3 defeat of Australia in the second leg of the tour. He was also on hand to guide Ireland to another Five Nations Championship in 1951, although the remainder of the decade wasn't as successful. He retired from international rugby in 1958 having played 46 times for his country and six times for the Lions. Six years later he hung up his club boots and began work on a humanitarian program in Indonesia and Sumatra. He also worked as a consultant surgeon for 35 years in Zambia.

In 2001 he returned to County Down and helped fund the Bursary scheme for the Queen's University Rugby Academy. In 2008 he was inducted into the IRB Hall of Fame.

Name: John Wilson 'Jack' Kyle, OBE
Born: 10th January 1926, Belfast
Home Union: Ireland
Position: Fly-half
Lions Tours: Australia & New Zealand (1950)
Number of Tests: 6
Points: 6

Laidlaw

Roy James Laidlaw played much of his rugby for Jed-Forest in the Scottish second division. He then appeared for the national B Team under Jim Telfer in the latter half of the 1970s. But he had to wait until 1980 before being given his first full cap against Ireland in the Five Nations (he'd been on the bench as an unused replacement for the previous ten games that season).

His patience was finally rewarded and he was ever-present with his half-back partner, John Rutherford, for the next three years. Laidlaw was then given the Scotland captaincy and he became known for terrorising opposition back rows with his breaks from the base of the scrum.

With Terry Holmes and Nigel Melville succumbing to injury, Laidlaw was called up for the 1983 Lions tour to New Zealand and he carried his outstanding form for Scotland into the Test series. He played in 13 of the 18 matches, captaining the side twice, and also featured in all four Tests, although the side was whitewashed.

He retired from international rugby in 1988 with 47 Scotland caps and four Lions appearances under his belt. It is for his world-record half-back partnership with John Rutherford and his devastating breaks that he will be best remembered.

Name: Roy James Laidlaw
Born: 5th October 1953, Jedburgh
Home Union: Scotland
Position: Scrum-half
Height / Weight: 5'6" (1.68cm) / 161lbs (73kg)
Lions Tours: New Zealand (1983)
Number of Tests: 4
Points: 0

Leonard

Leonard has been called rugby's Don Bradman and there's no doubt that the former Essex carpenter is a legend in his own lifetime. In a career that bridged the gap between the amateur and professional eras, Leonard was number one on the team sheet for 15 years.

He began his career at Barking before moving on to Saracens and then Harlequins in 1990. He became England's youngest prop at 21 in a brutal encounter against Argentina later that year, but he was then a regular in the side and racked up 40 consecutive caps, two Grand Slams and a World Cup final.

In 1993 he was selected for the Lions tour to New Zealand and earned a reputation as the 'song master' and a practical joker who helped the team bond. The team were soundly beaten by a strong Kiwi outfit, however, but another Grand Slam in 1995 saw his stock rise further. The World Cup later the same year saw him emerge from the disappointment of semi-final defeat to New Zealand with his head held high and he again toured with the Lions in South Africa on the glorious 1997 tour.

Another World Cup heartache in 1999 might have ushered lesser mortals into retirement but Leonard would enjoy an Indian summer to a special career. He was the dominant force in the Five Nations and on the 2001 Lions tour to Australia, and he rose to the occasion again as England secured a fourth Grand Slam in 2003.

LEONARD

Later in the year he became the most-capped player in the game's history (114 appearances), and he was on hand once more to steady the England ship when rocked by Australia in the World Cup final.

When he finally retired from one of the most physically demanding positions in the game in 2004, England coach Sir Clive Woodward led the tributes: "Jason has been an outstanding ambassador for the game on and off the pitch. His contribution towards four Grand Slams and the World Cup win has been incalculable."

Leonard then helped Harlequins to victory in the Parker Pen Challenge Cup before retiring from domestic rugby. He now works in the construction business, speaks on the after-dinner circuit and raises money for various charities.

Name: Jason Leonard, OBE
Born: 14th August 1968, London
Home Union: England
Position: Prop
Height / Weight: 5'10" (1.78m) / 245lbs (111kg)
Lions Tours: New Zealand (1993), South Africa (1997), Australia (2001)
Number of Tests: 5
Points: 0

Matthews

Matthews formed half of a legendary Welsh midfield with Bleddyn Williams. He was also a devastating tackler for such a small man. Born in Bridgend, South Wales, in 1920, Matthews attended the County School before heading for the University of Cardiff. He was short but powerfully built and quick, and he won the Welsh AAA 220 yards in 1937. A year later he was given a senior Welsh trial, and the year after that he came second in the Senior Men's 100 yards.

His career was interrupted by the war – which robbed him of his best years as an athlete – but he was commissioned into the medical corps and also learned to box. He famously held the future undefeated world champion Rocky Marciano to a draw and then resumed his rugby career with a win over France.

He played six Test matches for the Lions on the 1950 tour of Australia and New Zealand, earning the nicknames 'Iron Man', 'Bulldozer' and 'Brick Wall' for his brutal tackling and confrontational demeanour. He finished his international career in 1951 having been capped 17 times by Wales and six times by the Lions. He also joined the 1980 Lions on their tour of South Africa as the team doctor.

He maintained a healthy interest in sport after retiring from rugby and became medical officer to the Welsh Boxing Association. He died aged 92 in 2012.

Above: *Jack Matthews (right) touches down for a try*

Name: Jack Matthews, OBE
Born: 21st June 1920, Bridgend
Died: 18th July 2012
Home Union: Wales
Position: Centre
Height / Weight: 5'3" (1.61m) / 210lbs (93kg)
Lions Tours: Australia & New Zealand (1950)
Number of Tests: 6
Points: 0

McBride

Of all the players linked with the story of the Lions, one individual stands out; five times a tourist and leader of the most successful tour in their history: Willie John McBride. He is also the man who personified their famous team spirit, but it might have been so different. He was in his late teens before he considered rugby, but when he devoted his attention to the game his rise to superstardom was as quick as it was inevitable. At 21 he was an Ireland international and the following year he came on in the third and fourth Lions' Tests in South Africa.

The 1966 tour was less successful and the Lions were whitewashed by the All Blacks, but playing in all four Tests on the 1968 South Africa trip helped exorcise his demons and, with the emergence of the Welsh wizards, he knew the Lions had a bright future.

The lock hewn from the Ballymena granite eventually played in 17 Tests, although he endured nine straight defeats before tasting victory against the All Blacks in 1971. His appointment as pack leader during the trip saw an upsurge in the side's fortunes and he was selected as captain for the subsequent tour of South Africa on the back of four big performances.

The 1974 trip is perhaps the most famous in Lions history. The side were unbeaten throughout the 22-match tour, and they were determined never to take a backward step, even in the face of some brutal South African tactics. McBride adapted quickly and introduced the famous '99' call so that if any Lion thought they were in trouble, the rest of the Lions would rally round and get their retaliation in first.

He stands astride the legend of the Lions like a sporting colossus, and to this day Willie John remains the alpha male, leader of the pride.

Name: Willie John McBride, MBE
Born: 6th June 1940, Antrim
Home Union: Ireland
Position: Lock
Height / Weight: 6'3" (1.92m) / 225lbs (102kg)
Lions Tours: South Africa (1962), Australia & New Zealand (1966), South Africa (1968), New Zealand (1971), South Africa (1974), and as manager: New Zealand (1983)
Number of Tests: 17
Points: 3

McGeechan

Scotland's director of rugby, Ian McGeechan, belongs to a select band of warriors who have played for and coached the Lions. His record is phenomenal: a series win against South Africa as a player and series wins against Australia and South Africa as coach.

When the Leeds-born centre went on his first Lions tour to South Africa in 1974, he and Irish midfielder partner Dick Milliken were not the front-runners for the Test team because Geoff Evans and Roy Bergiers had been earmarked for the weekend side.

However, they both played their way into contention, with McGeechan's mazy running, deft hands, positional awareness and defence that belied his wiry physique endearing him to coach Syd Millar. It is testament to his impact on the side that he kept the great Mike Gibson on the bench when the latter arrived as a replacement. He was also extremely versatile and played five matches at stand-off half.

Three years later, McGeechan went to New Zealand and played in all four Tests, one of which was on the wing in place of the mercurial JJ Williams. He also captained the midweek side against Poverty Bay-East Coast and New Zealand Universities.

He transferred his success as a player into coaching and was chosen for the 1989 tour to Australia to instil the team with the awareness to beat the hosts. The Lions won the series 2-1

Above: *Ian McGeechan is unveiled as coach for the 2009 British and Irish Lions tour to South Africa*

having gone a game behind, and there's no doubt that McGeechan's tactical nous was partly responsible for the comeback.

Four years later, he was on the losing side in New Zealand, although the Lions did hammer the All Blacks in the second Test and only lost the first after the referee awarded the All Blacks a controversial last-minute penalty.

In 1997, McGeechan was back on hand to mastermind the Lions' victory in South Africa. The world champions may have been in decline but they were still expected to beat an inexperienced touring party comfortably. McGeechan again took charge of the side's preparation and he and fellow Scot Jim Telfer made sure the Lions were in the best physical and mental shape of their lives. Before they knew what had hit them, the Springboks were watching Matt Dawson scamper over for the try that won the first Test and Jerry Guscott slot the drop goal that sealed the series.

The Lions didn't have McGeechan's calmness and authority when they needed it most in 2001 but he was invited to tour New Zealand under Clive Woodward in 2005. It was not a successful trip, but he was on hand once more in 2009 to restore pride to the Lions in South Africa.

Name: Sir Ian Robert McGeechan, OBE
Born: 30th October 1946, Leeds
Home Union: Scotland
Position: Centre
Height / Weight: 5'9" (1.76m) / 156lbs (71kg)
Lions Tours: South Africa (1974), New Zealand (1977), and as coach: Australia (1989), New Zealand (1993), South Africa (1997), New Zealand (2005), South Africa (2009)
Number of Tests: 8
Points: 3

McLauchlan

When first-choice props Ray McLoughlin and Sandy Carmichael were injured during the glorified brawl in Canterbury on the 1971 Lions tour to New Zealand, the All Blacks believed the tourists' pack had been severely weakened, but understudies Ian McLauchlan and Sean Lynch stepped up to the plate and provided the platform for the Lions to win quality ball upfront and use their devastating backs to record their first series win over the Kiwis.

McLauchlan earned his 'Mighty Mouse' nickname by dismantling far bigger props through his body position, strength and technique, a tradition continued by compatriot Tom Smith against the Springboks in 1997. McLauchlan was unquestionably the model loose-head prop of his era and the textbook example for all props since. Because he wasn't carrying excess weight, he was also extremely mobile and he scored the decisive try in the first Test by forcing full-back Fergie McCormick into an error and then charging down Alan Sutherland's attempted clearance.

Three years later McLauchlan was captain of Scotland – he would eventually lead them to ten wins in 19 matches, both of which were records – and he was a cast-iron choice upfront for the tour to South Africa. The tourists' front row also included hooker Bobby Windsor and tight-head prop Fran Cotton, arguably one of the finest front rows ever assembled. McLauchlan made 13 appearances on the tour and captained the Lions

Left: *'Mighty Mouse' Ian McLauchlan may have been small by modern standards but the prop made up for his lack of size with superb technique*

against Southern Universities.

He led Scotland in the 1973 Calcutta Cup match with a broken bone in his leg and only retired in 1979 with 43 caps under his belt.

Name: Ian McLauchlan
Born: 14th April 1942, Tarbolton
Home Union: Scotland
Position: Prop
Height / Weight: 5'8" (1.73m) / 218lbs (99kg)
Lions Tours: New Zealand (1971), South Africa (1974)
Number of Tests: 8
Points: 3

McLeod

Hugh McLeod was a promising prop who was called up by Scotland in 1954 at the age of 21. The following year he was selected for the Lions tour to South Africa and earned a reputation as a hard man at the set-piece and in the loose. He was also extremely fit but he didn't manage to force his way into the Test side. He did publish a tour diary, however, that was refreshingly honest and well-received.

He returned to club side Hawick and continued his international career during the late 1950s. Legendary commentator Bill McLaren reckoned he was one of the best technicians and he was again selected for the Lions in 1959. This time he played in all six Tests, of which the tourists won three and lost three. He retired in 1962 after playing 40 times for his country and delivering several remarkable performances, which included a narrow defeat to the All Blacks at Murrayfield when he dominated the forward battle and nullified the mighty Kiwi front row.

Name: Hugh Ferns McLeod, OBE
Born: 8th June 1932, Hawick
Home Union: Scotland
Position: Prop
Height / Weight: 5'9" (1.75m) / 220lbs (100kg)
Lions Tours: South Africa (1955), Australia & New Zealand (1959)
Number of Tests: 6
Points: 0

McLoughlin

Ray McLoughlin played for Dublin University and then Blackrock College.

He was called up by Ireland in 1962 and soon earned a reputation as one of the game's great technicians. He wasn't big by modern standards but, like Ian McLauchlan and Tom Smith, he made up for this by using awkward body positions to subdue bigger opponents, and he was often voted the best loose-head prop in the business.

He toured with the Lions in 1966 and, although he played in three Tests, he picked up an injury that ruled him out of the decisive matches. In 1971 he was a casualty of the brawl in Canterbury and a broken thumb saw him sidelined after just five provincial matches. He probably would have played in the Test side but the Lions managed without him and won the series anyway. Despite also being a regular with the Barbarians, he retired from international rugby in 1975 with 40 Ireland caps and a try to his name.

Left: *Ray McLoughlin*

> **Name:** Raymond John McLoughlin
> **Born:** 24th August 1939, Ballinasloe
> **Home Union:** Ireland
> **Position:** Prop
> **Height / Weight:** 5'10" (1.78m) / 216lbs (98kg)
> **Lions Tours:** Australia & New Zealand (1966), New Zealand (1971)
> **Number of Tests:** 3
> **Points:** 3

Meredith, Bryn

As probably the most powerful, technically gifted, sure-handed and mobile hooker in rugby in the 1950s, South African pitches were made for Bryn Meredith. The Welshman thrived on his two tours, playing in eight Tests and scoring a record six tries by a hooker.

Meredith made his international debut for Wales in 1954 and became a Lion the following season. Over the next eight years he missed only three games for his country and went on another two tours with the Lions. The tourists shared the 1955 series with the Springboks, with Meredith, along with fellow front-rowers Billy Williams and Courtney Meredith, the catalyst for an outstanding – albeit losing – performance in the second Test in Cape Town. They may have been smaller than their opposite numbers but they were more mobile around the park and technically superior at the set-piece.

Meredith's reputation was enhanced by wining crucial strikes and popping up in the backline to take the try-scoring pass from centre Phil Davies. He proved himself again in 1959, although he had to compete with tour skipper Ronnie Dawson for a place in the Test team and only played in the provincial matches.

He captained the side against the Junior All Blacks but this was scant consolation, although he didn't complain and even popped up as a flanker when injuries forced a reshuffle on the Australian leg of the tour.

In 1962, Meredith was thought to have a good chance of skippering the tourists in South Africa but he missed out to Arthur Smith. He cemented his reputation by being picked for all four Tests and disrupting the Springbok forwards with his all-action style. He retired at the end of the tour with eight Lions and 34 Welsh caps, and he was voted Welsh sportsman of the year in his final season.

Name: Brinley 'Bryn' Victor Meredith
Born: 21st October 1930, Abersychan
Home Union: Wales
Position: Hooker
Height / Weight: 5'11" (1.80m) / 192lbs (87kg)
Lions Tours: South Africa (1955), Australia & New Zealand (1959), South Africa (1962)
Number of Tests: 8
Points: 3

Meredith, Courtney

Meredith played for club side Neath before being called up for international duty with Wales. He was a powerful and technical prop who gave his pack a solid foundation and allowed them to win good set-piece ball. He was selected for the 1955 Lions tour to South Africa and was part of the all-Wales front row that included Billy Williams and namesake but no relation Bryn Meredith. The closely fought series ended 2-2.

His international career may have been relatively short – 14 appearances and one try in four years for Wales is unremarkable – but Meredith's contribution to the game is far greater. He was the cornerstone of a Lions pack that nullified the Springboks in the first and third Tests, and the tourists eventually won 19 of their 25 games.

Name: Courtney Charles Meredith
Born: 23rd September 1926, Pontypridd
Home Union: Wales
Position: Prop
Height / Weight: 5'10" (1.78m) / 209lbs (95kg)
Lions Tours: South Africa (1955)
Number of Tests: 4
Points: 0

Millar

Not even the great Willie John McBride can match Syd Millar's Lions' record. He has been part of the side in some capacity for nearly half a century, playing on three tours, managing the team in South Africa in 1980, acting as chairman on the 2001 tour to Australia, selector in 1977, 1993 and 1997, and now as an active member on the rugby board that will oversee the 2013 Lions on their next Australian adventure.

The Ballymena and Ireland prop started playing at stand-off half but he grew too big for the position. Thankfully, he retained his ball skills and he was always a dangerous force in the loose. He first played for his country in 1958 and he toured with the Lions in 1959 and 1962. He was extremely versatile and could play on either side of the scrum, and he eventually played in 16 of the tourists' 24 matches on the latter tour. He was then, somewhat surprisingly, dropped by Ireland and had to wait another three years before winning the final 14 of his 37 caps and gaining selection for his third tour as a Lions player. He finally retired from international rugby in 1970.

He visited South Africa again in 1968 and returned as part of the coaching staff on the all-conquering 1974 tour, with Alun Thomas the standout member of his team. The 1980 trip presented a very different challenge given that the country was in the grip of apartheid and

the Lions came under close scrutiny for their attitude to the policy. Millar dealt with the issue superbly and allowed the team to do its talking on the pitch.

Millar rated the 1959 side as the best he ever played in, but the 1974 tour will be remembered as his finest hour with the Lions.

Name: Sydney 'Syd' Millar, CBE
Born: 23rd May 1934, Ballymena
Home Union: Ireland
Position: Prop
Height / Weight: 6'0" (1.83m) / 224lbs (102kg)
Lions Tours: Australia & New Zealand (1959), South Africa (1962 & 1968), as coach: South Africa (1974), and as manager: South Africa (1980)
Number of Tests: 9
Points: 0

Moore

A trained solicitor and qualified manicurist with a love of fine wine, opera and the classic French novel Germinal by Emile Zola, Brian Moore was an entirely different animal on the rugby field. Nicknamed 'pit bull', he was ferociously competitive and played with a passion and intensity that occasionally bent the rules. His combative attitude often detracted from the fact that he was the most technically proficient English hooker of his time, however.

Moore began his career at Nottingham, played his best rugby for Harlequins and ended up at Richmond. He was given a chance with the national team against Scotland during the 1987 Five Nations when Graham Dawe was suspended, and he only missed four of England's next 68 games. He brought his winner's attitude to the Lions squad in 1989, and, after helping the side to a 2-1 series win over Australia, he was famously spotted still celebrating on Sydney Harbour Bridge the following morning.

His growing influence within the England setup was reflected during the Grand Slam decider against Scotland at Murrayfield in 1990. Moore talked Will Carling into going for a pushover try instead of kicking a penalty. Scotland held out and took the championship in what was a devastating defeat for the auld enemy.

Moore had his revenge a year later when

Left: *Brian Moore*

victory over the Scots gave England their first Grand Slam since 1980. They also beat Scotland in the semi-final of the World Cup, but broke with tradition in the final against Australia when they tried to play a more expansive game. Moore was highly critical of this decision because he felt England's tried-and-tested forward-dominated game would have won them the trophy. He was still voted

Rugby World Player of the Year at the end of the tournament.

After another Grand Slam in 1992, Moore toured New Zealand with the Lions in 1993. During the second Test in Wellington, a can of beer was thrown onto the pitch. Moore had a quick drink before throwing it back to the fans. The Lions won the match after dominating the New Zealand pack but they lost the final game and with it the series.

Moore was at his abrasive best in the 1995 World Cup but the humiliating semi-final defeat to a Jonah Lomu-inspired All Blacks forced him to call time on a glittering career. Now an outspoken rugby commentator for the BBC, he also has a column with The Daily Telegraph, has written a best-selling autobiography and remains a popular speaker on the after-dinner circuit.

Name: Brian Christopher Moore	
Born: 11th January 1962, Birmingham	
Home Union: England	
Position: Hooker	
Height / Weight: 5'9" (1.76m) / 210lbs (95kg)	
Lions Tours: Australia (1989), New Zealand (1993)	
Number of Tests: 5	
Points: 0	

Morgan

If Tony O'Reilly was the star soloist for the 1955 Lions, Cliff Morgan was the conductor who called the tune. The South African media christened him 'Morgan the Magnificent' but the little Welshman had already earned his reputation as the finest stand-off in the country. Now he was able to unleash one of the greatest Lions backlines.

His blistering acceleration, a magical outside break and his elusive sidestep were his trademark, all of which were on show during the first Test, ranked by many as the greatest international ever played. The Lions were struggling after an injury to Reg Higgins reduced them to 14 men but Morgan broke from a scrum against the head and raced past Basie van Wyk to score the try that levelled the match.

With captain Robin Thompson injured before the decisive third Test, the Lions turned to Morgan for inspiration. He roused the side pre-match with a stirring speech and then proceeded to pen the Springboks in their own half with a series of pinpoint kicks. Victory by nine points to six meant the Lions could not lose the rubber, but their hopes of outright victory were dealt a blow when Morgan turned an ankle before the final Test. He played through the pain but he was a shadow of the maestro in the previous match and the Lions couldn't prevent South Africa squaring the series. The Welshman's reputation as the finest stand-off in the game was beyond doubt, however, and the South African press named him man of the series.

Morgan retired from top-class rugby in 1958 with 33 international appearances behind him. He then moved into broadcasting and journalism but was forced to retire when cancer of the vocal chords robbed him of the ability to speak. He was inducted into the IRB Hall of Fame in 2009.

Name: Clifford Isaac Morgan, OBE
Born: 7th April 1930, Trebanog
Home Union: Wales
Position: Fly-half
Height / Weight: 5'7" (1.71m) / 156lbs (71kg)
Lions Tours: South Africa (1955)
Number of Tests: 4
Points: 3

Above: *Cliff Morgan*

Mullen

Right: Karl Mullen laces up his boots before a big game

Educated at Belvedere College and the Royal College of Surgeons, Mullen played for Old Belvedere RFC. He earned the first of his 25 Ireland caps as a hooker against France in the 1947 Five Nations campaign, although he had previously played in uncapped games against France, England, Wales and Scotland in 1946.

Mullen took over his country's captaincy during the 1948 Five Nations Championship and with his laidback but determined style of play he guided the side to a famous Triple Crown and then to a historic first Grand Slam (he and the surviving members of that team witnessed Ireland's next Grand Slam in the 2009 Six Nations Championship).

He led the same side to a second Triple Crown in 1949 and was promptly selected as British & Irish Lions captain for the upcoming tour to Australia and New Zealand. He eventually played in 17 games on the tour, including three Test matches, of which he won one, drew one and lost one. He was injured for the final two Tests against the All Blacks and his leadership and ball skills were sorely missed. The Lions were much the weaker in his absence and lost the series.

He retired from international rugby with 25 Ireland caps, although he continued to play a role in the game and served as President of Leinster in 1963–64 as well as Chairman of the Irish selectors. Mullen died in 2009 after a long illness.

Name: Karl Daniel Mullen
Born: 26th November 1926, Courtown Harbour
Died: 26th April 2009
Home Union: Ireland
Position: Hooker
Lions Tours: Australia & New Zealand (1950)
Number of Tests: 3
Points: 0

Nicholls

Nicholls joined Cardiff in 1893 and remained with the club for the next 18

seasons, with four of those as club captain. The first of his 24 international appearances came against Scotland in 1896, but it was a solid if not spectacular debut. He was soon lighting up pitches with his pace and running lines, however, and he was selected for the 1899 tour to Australia. He played in all four Tests and scored two tries.

He returned to the Welsh side and captained them to the Triple Crown in 1902, and he was also at the helm for the historic win over the All Blacks in 1905. Following his retirement in 1906, he officiated at the England-Scotland match during the 1909 Home Unions Championship.

This prince of centres almost gave his own life while trying to rescue swimmers who had been caught in an undertow in Weston-super-Mare in 1923. He died in 1939 and was inducted into the International Rugby Hall of Fame in 2005.

Left: *Gwyn Nicholls*

Name: Erith Gwyn Nicholls
Born: 15th July 1874, Westbury-on-Severn
Died: 24th March 1939, Powys
Home Union: Wales
Position: Centre
Lions Tours: Australia (1899)
Number of Tests: 4
Points: 6

O'Callaghan

O'Callaghan

Right: Donncha O'Callaghan of Ireland wins the lineout ball

An abrasive and courageous lock, O'Callaghan has played more than 50 times for his country and he is renowned for his big hits in the loose and tireless graft. He represented Ireland at various junior levels and helped the side to the World Youth Championship in 1998 alongside future Ireland and Lions captain Brian O'Driscoll, as well as Paddy Wallace.

He made his international debut against Wales in a tight game at the Millennium Stadium in 2003 but he then struggled to hold down a place until selected by Clive Woodward for the 2005 Lions tour to New Zealand. The tour may not have been a great success but his partnership in the engine room with Paul O'Connell was one of the highlights and the pairing have now become a permanent fixture in the green of Ireland, as well as with Munster on the domestic front. He had a fabulous 2009 when he won the Grand Slam with Ireland and the Magners League with Munster, having also won Heineken Cups in 2006 and 2008.

The year was capped with selection for the 2009 Lions tour to South Africa and he had the honour of captaining the side against the Southern Kings, which ended with the tourists winning comfortably, 20-8. He came on as a replacement for Alun Wyn-Jones in the first Test in Durban but couldn't help the Lions salvage a late win. He was not included in the squads for the next two Tests.

He was ever-present for Ireland throughout 2009 and 2010, and he started every game at the 2011 World Cup. He earned his 90th cap against Argentina in 2012 and was included in the 2013 Six Nations squad.

Name: Donncha Fintan O'Callaghan
Born: 24th March 1979, Cork
Home Union: Ireland
Position: Lock
Height / Weight: 6'6" (1.98m) / 247lbs (112kg)
Lions Tours: New Zealand (2005), South Africa (2009)
Number of Tests: 4
Points: 0

O'Connell

O'Connell was a superb swimmer and rugby player at school. He played at youth levels for his country and finally made it into the senior squad for a match against Wales in the 2002 Six Nations. He scored a try on debut and was selected for the Rugby World Cup in 2003. The following year he stood in for the injured Brian O'Driscoll.

Sir Clive Woodward needed a towering presence in the pack to compete with Ali Williams, Brad Thorne and Chris Jack on the 2005 Lions tour to New Zealand and O'Connell was the obvious candidate. He played in every Test but the Lions couldn't compete with a dominant All Black pack and they were whitewashed in the series.

He then helped Ireland to the Triple Crown and was the only northern hemisphere nominee for the world player of the year. He captained the side once more in their historic demolition of England at Croke Park (43-13) in 2007, then captained club side Munster to European Cup glory.

He was again the standout lock on the 2009 Lions tour to South Africa, a role which saw him earn the captaincy and almost secure the series. The giant forward led Ireland at the 2011 World Cup and the 2012 Six Nations. He now has 85 caps and six tries for the national team under his belt, and has six appearances for the Lions. If he can avoid the knee injuries that have plagued the latter half of his career, he could provide a strong platform in Australia with the 2013 Lions.

Name: Paul Jeremiah O'Connell
Born: 20th October 1979, Limerick
Home Union: Ireland
Position: Lock
Height / Weight: 6'6" (1.98m) / 242lbs (110kg)
Lions Tours: New Zealand (2005), South Africa (2009)
Number of Tests: 6
Points: 0

Above: *Ireland's Paul O'Connell (left) tries to break through US players*

O'Driscoll

O'Driscoll is one of the most feared centres in world rugby. Blessed with great strength, a brutal hand-off, devastating sidestep, good flat speed and a bone-shaking tackle, he is one of the few players who would walk into any side in the game.

He was born in Dublin and initially gravitated to Gaelic Football but a spell at Blackrock College convinced him to pursue rugby and he made the senior cup team in 1996, a year in which he was also capped by Ireland Schools. He joined Leinster in 1999 and helped the side to the semi-final of the 2003 European Cup.

His good early form for the club's Second XV saw him selected for Ireland in a humbling 46-10 defeat to Australia. In 2000 he lit up the international stage with a hat-trick against France in Paris, and, the following year, he had his personal revenge over Australia when he scored a fabulous individual try for the Lions at the Gabba that ensured the tourists won the first Test. They couldn't take the series, however, so he guided Ireland to a first win over the Wallabies since 1979.

More success with club and country followed and he was the only realistic choice as captain for the 2005 Lions tour to New Zealand. His tour ended just two minutes into the first Test however when he was spear tackled by Tana Umaga and Keven Mealamu and aggravated an old shoulder injury. It was a sad end to what could have been a terrific series for the Irishman, although it's doubtful whether his presence alone would have been enough to see off a strong All Black side.

He was back to his blistering and combative best in the first Test of the 2009 series against South Africa when he provided two assists, but the Lions ran out of steam and went down 26-21. He was concussed in the second match and missed the third Test. With 127 international caps, 47 tries and 250 points in the bank, O'Driscoll is one of the modern game's true greats, and Will Carling placed him in the top ten of all time. He was back to his best in the first game of the 2013 Six Nations Championship and could yet tour with the 2013 Lions.

> **Name:** Brian Gerald O'Driscoll,
> **Born:** 21st January 1979, Dublin
> **Home Union:** Ireland
> **Position:** Centre
> **Height / Weight:** 5'10" (1.78m) / 205lbs (93kg)
> **Lions Tours:** Australia (2001), New Zealand (2005), South Africa (2009)
> **Number of Tests:** 6
> **Points:** 5

O'Reilly

As a teenager, it only took Anthony O'Reilly five senior appearances to play his way into the Ireland team. Four matches later, he was called up for the 1955 Lions tour to South Africa. He promptly broke the tourists' try-scoring record but, as a wing with lightning acceleration and a devastating sidestep, Tony O'Reilly always seemed to be in a hurry. If the tour made his reputation, his 15 tries in 16 games – including two in the Test series – cemented his legend.

Although Barry John was treated like pop royalty in 1971, O'Reilly was the sport's first superstar. On the 1959 trip to New Zealand he destroyed his own scoring record, which, given the different circumstances of today's tours, is unlikely to be beaten. He ran in 22 tries in 24 matches, including four in the Tests, one in each international against Australia and two more against the All Blacks.

O'Reilly loved the freedom he found with the Lions that he didn't have with Ireland. With the world's best players inside him he saw much more of the ball and he loved to play on the gain line, coming on to the ball at full speed 10 or 15 times in a game. The Lions played beautiful running rugby and O'Reilly was perhaps the finest runner in the game's history.

Above: *Tony O'Reilly (left) on the charge against the Junior All Blacks in 1959*

Name: Sir Anthony Joseph Francis O'Reilly
Born: 7th May 1936, Dublin
Home Union: Ireland
Position: Wing
Height / Weight: 6'2" (1.88m) / 206lbs (94kg)
Lions Tours: South Africa (1955), Australia & New Zealand (1959)
Number of Tests: 10
Points: 18

PASK

Pask

Alun Pask went to Loughborough University and made his debut for Wales in 1961, scoring a try in their match against Ireland. The following year he was selected to tour with the Lions and played in three of the four Tests against South Africa. Although the series wasn't a great success, he was again on the team-sheet for the next tour to Australia and New Zealand.

In the Five Nations before the tour he was selected as captain and Wales duly lifted the trophy. He then played in both the wins over the Wallabies and three of the four unsuccessful games against the All Blacks. He retired from international rugby the following year having racked up 26 appearances and two tries for Wales and eight starts for the Lions.

Name: Alun Edward Islwyn Pask
Born: 10th September 1937, Blackwood
Died: 1st November 1995
Home Union: Wales
Position: Number 8
Height / Weight: 6'2" (1.88m) / 198lbs (90kg)
Lions Tours: South Africa (1962), Australia & New Zealand (1966)
Number of Tests: 8
Points: 0

Price

Graham Price played in 12 successive matches for the Lions and he became the tourists' most-capped prop. His power and technique made him the game's most respected front-row forward.

He made his Wales debut in 1975 alongside Pontypool stalwarts Bobby Windsor and Charlie Faulkner. Two years later, the same three men would dominate the Lions front row in tour matches against Counties, Bay of Plenty and Fiji. Price confirmed his status on the 1977 New Zealand tour as a prop of considerable ability in what was perhaps the strongest front five the game had yet seen. He withstood everything the All Blacks threw at him and was selected on the back of more good performances in the red of Wales for his second Lions tour in 1980.

He again fronted up to the Springbok pack in all four Tests and proved himself technically superior to the hosts, even scoring a try after a strong eight-man shove. He was also proficient in the loose, and his handling and timing of the pass from contact allowed the speedsters to make use of the extra time and space he afforded them.

By 1983 his career was winding down and, although selected for the tour to New Zealand, the Lions suffered a 4-0 series defeat. With the respect he deserved from the public, he retired from international rugby at the end of the tour.

He racked up 41 caps for Wales and 12 for the Lions, both then records for a prop, with the latter unlikely to be broken now that tours are limited to three Tests.

Above: *Graham Price pictured during the Second Test match between New Zealand and the British Lions*

Name: Graham Price
Born: 24th November 1951, Moascar, Egypt
Home Union: Wales
Position: Prop
Height / Weight: 6'0" (1.83m) / 210lbs (95kg)
Lions Tours: New Zealand (1977), South Africa (1980), New Zealand (1983)
Number of Tests: 12
Points: 4

Pullin

John Pullin was an inspirational captain who won everything in the game prior to the establishment of the World Cup. Victories over the any of the southern hemisphere superpowers are rare but Pullin oversaw victories over all three, a feat not repeated until Martin Johnson took over 20 years later.

A farmer from Aust in the West Country, Pullin made his name in the impressive Bristol side of the 1960s. The hooker made his debut for England in 1966 and he was such an influence on the team that he was selected to tour South Africa with the Lions two years later. He was also chosen to join the immortal Lions in New Zealand in 1971 in what was a glorious period for European rugby.

Having won the series convincingly, Pullin then guided England to the treble, starting with an 18-9 victory over the Springboks at Ellis Park in 1972. He also masterminded victory over the All Blacks in Auckland before Australia succumbed at Twickenham. The win in New Zealand was perhaps the most significant as no England team had won there before.

Pullin captained his country 13 times, and his record of 42 caps at hooker stood until Brian Moore overhauled it in 1993. He was also the only Englishman to feature in the most famous try in the history of rugby when the Barbarians counterattacked against New Zealand from deep in their own 25 at the Arms Park and ended with Gareth Edwards scoring in the opposite corner. Phil Bennett may have started the move but slick hands from Pullin, John Dawes, Tom David and Derek Quinnell ensured that the ball ended up where it needed to be: with Edwards at full steam 40 yards out.

Name: John Vivian Pullin
Born: 1st November 1941, Gloucestershire
Home Union: England
Position: Hooker
Height / Weight: 6'0" (1.83m) / 212lbs (96kg)
Lions Tours: South Africa (1968), New Zealand (1971)
Number of Tests: 7
Points: 0

Quinnell

Quinnell was educated in Llanelli and joined his local club in 1967. He made such an impression that he was selected for the Lions tour to New Zealand in 1971 without having been capped by Wales. He played in the third Test on the successful tour and made his debut for Wales in the Five Nations the following season.

He eventually won 23 caps for his country and was again selected for the Lions. He made two Test appearances in New Zealand in 1977 and another two in South Africa three years later. All three of his sons played top-flight rugby, with Craig playing for Wales 32 times and scoring five tries, Scott being capped by his country (52 times with 11 tries) and by the Lions (three times with one try against Australia in 2001), and Gavin playing for the Scarlets.

Name: Derek Leslie Quinnell
Born: 22nd May 1949, Llanelli
Home Union: Wales
Position: Number 8
Height / Weight: 6'4" (1.92m) / 231lbs (105kg)
Lions Tours: New Zealand (1971 & 1977), South Africa (1980)
Number of Tests: 5
Points: 0

Above: *Derek Quinnell in action*

Left: *Derek Quinnell*

Richards

Deano was an old-school big-game player who, despite his rather plodding and ungainly appearance, was one of the finest forwards in the game's history. He was an absolute master of turning ball over, giving his backs a platform from which to counterattack, and putting in the hard yards upfront. He was often overlooked by coaches wanting to play a more expansive game, but you can't play rugby without the ball and to win quality possession you needed Richards. The fact that he was on the losing side only four times in his last 29 internationals proves his value to the England setup.

Richards worked his way into the Leicester XV in the early 1980s. He made his debut for England against Ireland in 1986, scoring two tries in a 25-20 win. Although still considered a fringe player, the following year he made the first World Cup squad and played four times for a hapless England. He cemented his position in the side during the next Five Nations campaign and he was rewarded with selection for the 1989 Lions tour to Australia. They lost the first Test but with Mike Teague returning to the side, the back row (Richards, Teague and Finlay Calder) was unstoppable and the Lions sealed a 2-1 series win.

How England could have done with Richards at Murrayfield for the Grand Slam decider against Scotland in 1990, but the big policeman was injured and the Scottish back row gave their backs enough ball to stifle the English attack.

The following year he teamed up with Teague and Peter Winterbottom in one of the game's most formidable back rows. England promptly won back-to-back Grand Slams and made the final of the 1991 World Cup. However, a tactical rethink saw him replaced by Mickey Skinner before the final, but the move backfired. England couldn't control the ball the way they had in the pool games and lost 12-6 to Australia.

Jack Rowell dropped him but the Lions couldn't do without him and he earned another three caps in New Zealand in 1993. It was a disappointing tour, however, and the Lions were comprehensively outplayed in the decisive third Test in Auckland.

Another Grand Slam and solid showing at the World Cup in 1995 proved what an asset Richards was, and he backed this up on the domestic front by captaining Leicester to the Courage League Championship. He played his last game for England in 1996 before switching to coaching. Back-to-back Heineken Cups and four successive Premiership titles followed – not bad for a man who some thought was out of touch

with the modern game. He ended a 24-year association with Leicester when he joined Grenoble in 2004 and then NEC Harlequins.

His formidable reputation was undermined by the 'bloodgate' scandal in which he asked players to fake injuries, but, having served his ban, Richards returned to coaching with the Newcastle Falcons and may well be a candidate for the England job in the future.

Name: Dean Richards, MBE
Born: 11th July 1963, Nuneaton
Home Union: England
Position: Number 8
Height / Weight: 6'3" (1.91m) / 267lbs (121kg)
Lions Tours: Australia (1989), New Zealand (1993)
Number of Tests: 6
Points: 0

Robinson

When rugby union turned professional in 1995 it was inevitable that some players would defect from rugby league. Many came but few succeeded. The exception was former Wigan wing Jason Robinson. He cemented his reputation as one of the game's deadliest finishers when he scored England's only try in the 2003 World Cup final.

Born in Leeds, Robinson had a record-breaking rugby league career (302 appearances and 685 points) with Wigan. Nicknamed Billy Whizz for his darting runs and devastating sidestep, he was also an integral member of the Great Britain rugby league side along with legends like Ellery Hanley, Martin Offiah and Shaun Edwards. In 1996 he made a temporary switch and joined Bath but he returned to his original code to help Wigan win Super League's first grand final in 1998.

The diminutive winger completed a rare double when, having signed for union outfit Sale in 2000, he was then selected for the 2001 Lions tour to Australia having not made a start for England. He was the find of the series, however, scoring a blistering solo try to defeat the Aussies in the first Test and another that almost won the third Test in Sydney.

Robinson was a regular in the England team that swept all before them in 2002-03, and he was again selected for the Lions on the 2005 tour to New Zealand. It was not a happy tour for the Lions, however, and they were soundly beaten. He was offered the England captaincy for the autumn internationals, thus becoming the first mixed race player and the first former rugby league player to take the role. He scored a hat-trick against Canada in his first game in charge but he retired from international rugby in September having led Sale to their first English title.

Robinson was coaxed out of retirement by Brian Ashton before the 2007 World Cup but he was injured in their first game – a heavy defeat to eventual champions South Africa – and sat out the remaining pool games. He returned to help England squeeze past Australia and led the side out for the semi-final against France. His last match for his country was the final, which England narrowly lost.

He came out of retirement for a season with Fylde but hung up his boots for good in 2011.

Name: Jason Thorpe Robinson
Born: 30th July 1974, Leeds, Yorkshire
Home Union: England
Position: Wing / fullback
Height / Weight: 5'8" (1.73m) / 179lbs (81kg)
Lions Tours: Australia (2001), New Zealand (2005)
Number of Tests: 5
Points: 10

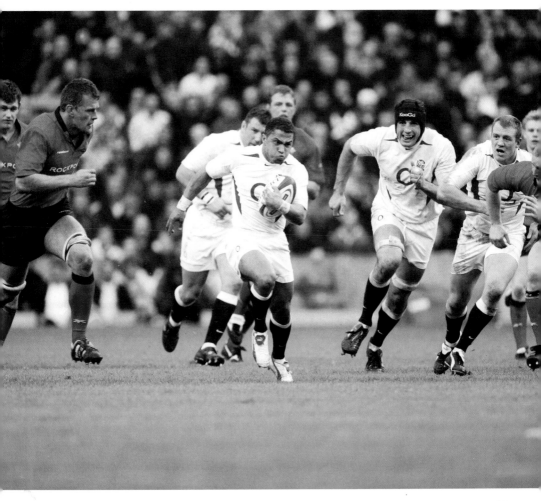

Rodber

Right: *Tim Rodber (centre) of Northampton lift the trophy after the Heineken Cup Final*

England enjoyed a golden era in the 1990s and their success was largely due to a surplus of talented back-row forwards like Dean Richards, Ben Clarke, Peter Winterbottom, Mike Teague and Mickey Skinner. Green Howards' army officer Tim Rodber began his England career at No.8 but he switched to blindside flanker when Lawrence Dallaglio arrived on the scene.

Rodber was a skilled forward at school and he joined Northampton in 1987. He rose through the ranks and made his England debut against Scotland in their Grand Slam-winning 1992 season. He played alongside Matt Dawson and Dallaglio in England's 1993 World Cup sevens team and was ever-present for the full side throughout 1994. He did, however, manage to get himself sent off for fighting against Eastern Province during the tour to South Africa.

He played a key role in the 1995 Grand Slam and World Cup season and was unlucky not to be selected more consistently thereafter. He returned to the fold for the 1997 Five Nations and was selected on the back of a good domestic season to tour with the Lions later that year. He earned two caps in the successful series but injury ruled him out of the start of the Woodward era. He came back again, however, and was partnered with Martin Johnson in the engine room for the 1999 Five Nations.

He was made Saints captain in 1994, a post

he held for five years under Ian McGeechan's management. The side didn't have huge success but Rodber ended his career on a high when they lifted the European Cup at Twickenham after edging out Munster in 2000. He retired at the end of the following season and is now CEO of Williams Lea after a successful period at the helm of international operations.

Name: Timothy Andrew Keith Rodber
Born: 2nd July 1969, Richmond, Yorkshire
Home Union: England
Position: Number 8, Flanker, Lock
Height / Weight: 6'6" (1.98m) / 245lbs (111kg)
Lions Tours: South Africa (1997)
Number of Tests: 2
Points: 0

Scotland

Ken Scotland was a superb all-round sportsman who played international cricket and could fill in just about anywhere on the rugby pitch. He was also the one player who pioneered the art of coming into the line at pace from full-back and giving the attack an extra option. JPR Williams and Andy Irvine may also be remembered for practising the art but Scotland got there 20 years earlier.

The Scottish international was ever-reliable on the 1959 Lions tour, both in attack and defence. The timing and pace of his incursions into the backline, allied with a change of gear that could break any defensive system, allowed him to glide through gaps in much the same way that Jeremy Guscott would for England in the 1980s and 1990s. He scored 12 tries in 22 appearances on the tour – including a hat-trick in the opening match against Hawkes Bay and a spectacular solo effort that won the game against Bay of Plenty. The side won the final Test and the New Zealand Rugby Almanac rated him as the most likely player to win a match. The publication also named him as one of its five players of the year, along with fellow tourists Bev Risman, Rhys Williams and Terry Davies.

As well as being the supreme counter-attacking full-back of the post-war era, Scotland was also a fine defensive kicker from hand and also helped introduce the round-the-corner style of place-kicking that has since become the accepted technique.

Left: *Ken Scotland*

Name: Kenneth J. F. Scotland
Born: 29th August 1936, Edinburgh
Home Union: Scotland
Position: Full-back
Height / Weight: 5'10" (1.78m) / 156lbs (71kg)
Lions Tours: Australia & New Zealand (1959)
Number of Tests: 5
Points: 8

Shaw

Shaw represented England at various junior levels and joined Bristol a year after taking up the sport seriously. In 1997 he joined London Wasps and solid performances saw him selected for both England and the Lions. He was never going to oust Martin Johnson or Jeremy Davidson from the Test side but he was a tough, no-nonsense stalwart of the midweek side and their success undoubtedly contributed to the feel-good factor on the tour.

A number of injuries hampered his progress and he struggled to hold down a permanent place in the England team. The side was particularly strong in the second row with Johnson, Steve Borthwick and Danny Grewcock competing for places so it is a measure of his talent and longevity that he still won 71 caps for his country. He played in the big three build-up matches to the 2003 World Cup but didn't play a Test at the tournament.

When Malcolm O'Kelly aggravated an injury, Clive Woodward had no hesitation in calling Shaw into the 2005 Lions squad for the tour to New Zealand. He wasn't first choice for the Tests and the Lions arguably missed his ball-winning in the loose and his ferocious defensive tacking. He was on hand during the 2007 World Cup and played in the final itself. Two years later he went on his third Lions tour as the oldest player ever to be selected. He proved the doubters who believed he was past his best

wrong by putting in a huge performance in the second Test. Although the Lions lost the Test and the series, he was voted man-of-the-match for what has since been called the greatest game by a British & Irish lock.

He was in the England squad for the 2011 World Cup and now plays his rugby in Toulon.

Name: Simon Dalton Shaw, MBE
Born: 1st September 1973, Nairobi
Home Union: England
Position: Lock
Height / Weight: 6'8" (2.03m) / 269lbs (122kg)
Lions Tours: South Africa (1997), New Zealand (2005), South Africa (2009)
Number of Tests: 2
Points: 0

Slattery

With Roger Uttley and Mervyn Davies, Fergus Slattery was the final piece in a back-row jigsaw that is still considered the best in the game. They dominated the breakdown and blitzed the Springbok defence to help the tourists claim their famous series win over South Africa in 1974.

Slattery made his name three years earlier, however, when in New Zealand with the 1971 Lions. As a 22-year-old, the Blackrock College player had only just made his Ireland debut but he played his way into the team for the third Test. Sadly he was then sidelined on the morning of the game with a fever.

Despite suffering concussion and losing two teeth in the infamous Battle of Canterbury, Slattery played in 12 of the 24 matches and earned favourable comparisons with Irish legend Bill McKay who had been the standout player on the 1950 tour.

He dominated games from open-side flanker with his physical and abrasive style, his punishing pace and his eye for a gap. At the breakdown he was peerless, recycling ball that he had no right to win, and ensuring that the Lions could mount more attacks than they would have otherwise. Indeed he should have been awarded a try in the final Test of the 1974 tour that would have given the visitors a 4-0 series whitewash. The scores were level at 13-13 when Slattery touched down but the

referee hadn't seen him ground the ball and in the days before video evidence he couldn't award the try. He then blew for fulltime before the Lions could attack from the five-yard scrum.

Slattery finally retired from international rugby after 14 years with 61 caps.

Above: *Fergus Slattery slips a tackle on the 1971 Lions tour to New Zealand*

> Name: John Fergus Slattery
> Born: 12th February 1949, Dún Laoghaire
> Home Union: Ireland
> Position: Flanker
> Height / Weight: 6'1" (1.85m) / 205lbs (93kg)
> Lions Tours: New Zealand (1971), South Africa (1974)
> Number of Tests: 4
> Points: 0

Smith, Arthur

Arthur Smith was a superb all-round athlete who had been national long-jump champion, and he made a spectacular start to his international career in 1955 when he helped his side end a depressing run of 17 straight defeats with a spectacular solo try against Wales. The game would forever be remembered as 'Arthur Smith's match'. This magnificent wing would also be given the Lions captaincy for their tour to South Africa in 1962.

His good form saw him initially selected for the Lions in South Africa in 1955 but he broke his hand in the first match and only made three more appearances on the tour. Seven years later the Lions were back in South Africa with Smith as captain. The Galloway-born wing had led his country 15 times and the Lions were tipped to do well in the southern hemisphere but the 1962 side couldn't match the achievements of their predecessors. Smith's personal contribution was never in doubt however, as he made enough of the ball he did receive to score eight tries. He was injured for the final match of the 1962 tour and that turned out to be his international swansong, although he was a great servant to the game in retirement and introduced coaching camps that would help the team prepare for the incredible tours of the 1970s.

He ended his career with the remarkable record of 33 tries in 33 internationals, his smooth running style and scorching pace getting him out of many a tight spot. He died of cancer in 1975 aged only 42.

Name: Arthur Robert Smith
Born: 23rd January 1933, Castle Douglas
Died: 3rd February 1975
Home Union: Scotland
Position: Wing
Height / Weight: 6'0" (1.83m) / 176lbs (80kg)
Lions Tours: South Africa (1955 & 1962)
Number of Tests: 3
Points: 0

Smith, Tom

Above: *Tom Smith delivers a pass from the base of the ruck*

The giant Kiwi and Springbok forwards licked their lips when pint-sized Ian McLauchlan was drafted into the Lions front row in 1971 and 1974, but 'Mighty Mouse' gave them a lesson in technical scrummaging and secured so much ball for the tourists that they won both series. The massive Springbok front row and the enormous media presence had clearly forgotten the lesson from the past because when they saw Tom Smith's name on the team-sheet for the 1997 series they again predicted a comfortable win.

History of course repeated itself. Despite giving away several stone in weight and six inches in height to Adrian Garvey and Os du Randt, Smith and the equally diminutive but equally mobile and technically gifted Paul Wallace used awkward body positions to give the Springboks a scrummaging master-class which destabilized their entire pack. This meant that Joost van der Westhuizen, Percy Montgomery and Henry Honiball didn't get the quick ball their backs needed from the set-piece or in the loose and the Lions dominated upfront.

Although this was Smith's first season in international rugby and he only had three caps to his name, his mobility and skill made him an ideal choice for the high-speed game coaches Ian McGeechan and Jim Telfer wanted to play. Victory in the first two Tests were built on the solid foundations of the Smith–Wood–Wallace axis, and Smith was an automatic choice for the Lions on the 2001 trip to Australia. He was again the outstanding prop in both sides, although he couldn't prevent the tourists losing the last match and conceding the series 2-1.

Smith retired from international rugby in 2005 with 67 caps and six international tries to his name, and it came as no surprise that he was voted the greatest prop ever to have played in the World Cup in a poll in 2007. His performances with the Lions on the glorious 1997 tour only enhanced this reputation.

He retired from club rugby in 2009 but now works as a forwards' coach with Lyon.

Name: Thomas James 'Tom' Smith
Born: 31st October 1971, London
Home Union: Scotland
Position: Prop
Height / Weight: 5'10" (1.78m) / 227lbs (103kg)
Lions Tours: South Africa (1997), Australia (2001)
Number of Tests: 6
Points: 0

SQUIRE

Squire

Right: *Jeff Squire*
Below: *Jeff Squire releases the ball from a maul*

Squire captained St Luke's before moving to Cross Keys RFC. He served his apprenticeship with Newbridge, Newport and Pontypool before being called up to the Welsh squad in 1977. He played in two matches of that year's Five Nations campaign and made enough of an impact to be selected for the Lions tour to New Zealand later that year.

It proved to be a tough series but he featured in a couple of the Tests. His form with Wales was outstanding the following year and he helped them to a Grand Slam with emphatic victories over the home unions and France. In 1980 he toured South Africa but the Lions were again outplayed, as indeed they were back in New Zealand in 1983. Professionalism had been creeping into southern hemisphere rugby and the north simply couldn't cope with the power and pace of the All Blacks.

Name: Jeffrey Squire
Born: 23rd September 1951, Pontywaun
Home Union: Wales
Position: Flanker, Number 8
Height / Weight: 6'3" (1.91m) / 214lbs (97kg)
Lions Tours: New Zealand (1977), South Africa (1980), New Zealand (1983)
Number of Tests: 6
Points: 0

Taylor

Taylor was born in Watford and played for London Welsh. He won his first cap for Wales in 1967 at the age of 21 and then played 26 Tests during the golden era of Welsh rugby in the 1970s. His greatest moment for his country came during a Five Nations game against Scotland in 1971. With regular kicker Barry John out with concussion, he slotted a conversion from the touchline to secure a dramatic one-point win.

He toured with the Lions in 1968 and again in 1971, although he played no Tests on his first tour. In the second, he played in all four Tests and helped the Lions beat the All Blacks for the only time in the tourists' history. He refused to tour South Africa in the apartheid era and wouldn't even play the Springboks when they visited the UK in 1969-70.

He retired in 1978 and began a successful career in broadcasting and journalism, notably with ITV where he was the lead at several World Cups and also called England's dramatic 2003 win over Australia in the final. He's now a regular behind the microphone for talkSport radio.

Left: *John Taylor in action.*

Name: John Taylor
Born: 21st July 1945, Watford
Home Union: Wales
Position: Flanker
Height / Weight: 5'11" (1.80m) / 189lbs (86kg)
Lions Tours: South Africa (1968), New Zealand (1971)
Number of Tests: 4
Points: 0

Teague

'Iron Mike' was another no-nonsense West Country forward who played for Gloucester and Moseley in the 1980s, and was a key member of the England back row that helped them to the Grand Slam and the World Cup final in 1991.

He cut his teeth in bruising top-flight encounters before making his England debut in a 9-9 draw with France at Twickenham in 1985. He then went on the national team's tour to New Zealand but was inexplicably overlooked for the next three years. He fought his way back into contention during 1989 but his career was by no means assured until he was selected for the Lions tour to Australia that winter.

The Lions were outplayed in the first Test but Teague started the last two matches and was named man of the series after his heroic performances. It was the first time a touring party had gone behind in a series before coming back to win.

He played three matches in the 1990 Five Nations but England missed out on the Grand Slam after being outplayed by Scotland at Murrayfield. The following year would see a change in their fortunes: the back row obliterated the Welsh at the Cardiff Arms Park and Teague scored the only try of the game. More solid performances helped England to the Grand Slam and World Cup final, although a change in tactics in the latter probably cost them the Webb Ellis Trophy.

He was injured for much of 1992 and only managed one Test (a big win against South Africa). He then had to wait until 1993 for his next cap but the Five Nations campaign was disappointing. Although the Lions lost the 1993 series in New Zealand, it's no coincidence that Teague played in the only Test the tourists' won, ensuring his 100% record with the Lions.

He now runs a couple of pubs and a property development business.

Name: Michael Clive Teague
Born: 8th October 1960, Gloucester
Home Union: England
Position: Flanker
Height / Weight: 6'3" (1.90m) / 234lbs (106kg)
Lions Tours: Australia (1989), New Zealand (1993)
Number of Tests: 3
Points: 0

Telfer

Along with coaching partner Ian McGeechan, Jim Telfer is a Scots legend whose contribution to the Lions can't be quantified. The former Melrose number eight toured twice as a player, once as head coach and once more as McGeechan's assistant.

Telfer made 22 appearances on the 1966 Lions tour to Australia and New Zealand, playing both on the flank and at eight and earning a reputation as a combative but fair player of considerable talent and grit. After the bloodbath at Canterbury, in which he had captained the tourists, he defied the team management and told the press exactly what he thought about the violence his team had been subjected to. Despite initial antipathy towards him for speaking out, he was a man of character who was begrudgingly respected for taking such a vehement stance against foul play.

Telfer was carrying an injury in 1968 but he still led the Lions pack in 11 of 20 matches and his abrasive and outspoken style again earned him the respect of the Springboks, particularly during the backs-to-the-wall effort that secured the tourists a draw in the second Test.

He was equally combative as a coach and his punishing schedules often reduced seasoned campaigners to tears. A packed itinerary, injury to several key players and superior opposition limited his achievements in 1983 and the team was whitewashed by the All Blacks.

Fourteen years later Telfer's fitness drills and defensive patterns were finally vindicated during the first professional tour to South Africa. He was the heart and soul of the coaching outfit and his team talks were so compelling that many of the tourists were almost overcome with emotion. The team translated this into a potent weapon, however, and Telfer's commitment, drive and tactical nous helped guide them to a historic series win over the world champions.

Name: James 'Jim' Telfer
Born: 17 March 1940, Melrose
Home Union: Scotland
Position: Number 8
Height / Weight: 6'2" (1.88m) / 206lbs (94kg)
Lions Tours: Australia & New Zealand (1966), South Africa (1968), and as coach: New Zealand (1983), South Africa (1997)
Number of Tests: 6
Points: 0

Thomas

Right: *Another line-out to the British Lions as Delme Thomas (right) climbs above New South Wales' Owen Butler*

It was a controversial decision to select uncapped Welsh lock Delme Thomas for the 1966 Lions tour to New Zealand when there were several internationally accomplished rivals in the mix. When the tourists returned, however, his inclusion was viewed as one of the management's few good decisions.

Thomas played against the All Blacks on their tour of the British Isles in 1963. He'd been impressed with their physicality and dominance at the set-piece so he bulked up and improved his lineout skills. Three years later he was deputizing for the incomparable Rhys Williams at Stradey Park, Llanelli, and he immediately justified his selection on the tour to New Zealand by taking tour captain Mike Campbell-Lamerton's place for the second Test. With the captain reinstated for the third match, the management found room for Thomas at prop, an unprecedented move that only enhanced his reputation within the squad.

He again played in the front row on the 1968 tour to South Africa, although by now he was firmly established in the Welsh side. He twice faced up to the mighty Springbok forwards, coming on as a replacement in the third Test and starting the fourth. He still hadn't been on the winning side but the team was in transition and only reaped the rewards on the 1971 tour to New Zealand. He was again in the midst of the action, appearing in three of the four Tests and playing an important role in the series-opening win. He eventually played in 14 of the 24 tour matches before returning and getting the last of his 25 caps with Wales. He retired from international rugby in 1974.

Name: Delme Thomas
Born: 12th September 1942, Carmarthen
Home Union: Wales
Position: Lock, Prop
Height / Weight: 6'2" (1.88m) / 222lbs (101kg)
Lions Tours: New Zealand (1966), South Africa (1968), New Zealand (1971)
Number of Tests: 7
Points: 0

Underwood

This electrifying Leicester winger really could fly. A trained RAF fighter pilot, Underwood brought his speed and reactions to the England setup and raced over for a record 49 tries in 85 appearances (fifth on the all-time list). He was also the first England player to win 50 caps.

Underwood played alongside Rob Andrew at Barnard Castle School before entering the RAF's officer training program. He continued playing during his air force days and, having joined Leicester Tigers in what was still an amateur period for the sport, he was called up for England in 1984 for their Five Nation encounter with Ireland at Twickenham.

He initially struggled in a team that didn't give him much ball and it wasn't until Geoff Cooke took over as England coach that he played with a newfound freedom and his international career took off. With his electric acceleration and ability to feint off either foot at top speed, he conjured countless tries from seemingly impossible situations. He scored five against Fiji in 1989, equalling an 82-year-old record for the most scored in an international, and this secured him a berth on the 1989 Lions tour to Australia. He racked up another four tries in eight games as the Lions won 2-1.

Two years earlier his World Cup had ended in disappointment, but England were a team in transition and they were building towards a

Above: *Rory (left) and Tony Underwood hold the Calcutta Cup and the Five Nations Trophy*

golden era. Underwood scored crucial tries in the 1990, 1991 and 1992 Five Nations championships and helped steer England to a World Cup final showdown with Australia. For once, he saw a lot of the ball but the Aussie defence kept him quiet and held on to take the match.

His brother joined him in the team in 1992 and they gained revenge over Australia in the quarter-final of the 1995 World Cup – a Five Nations Grand Slam was already in the bag –

but neither Underwood could cope with Lomu and England bowed out meekly after semi-final defeat to the All Blacks. His 11 tries in 15 World Cup matches see him ranked third overall behind only Lomu and fellow Kiwi Doug Howlett.

The two Grand Slams in the early 1990s saw him called up for the Lions tour to New Zealand and he raced past John Kirwan to score one of the tries in the second Test that helped the tourists to victory. They lost the final Test but Underwood's good form continued. In 1996 he racked up ten consecutive Five Nations Championships without missing a match. He then retired from international rugby, although he did help Leicester to two championships

before hanging up his boots for good.

Underwood is now a management consultant, occasional model for the RAF's new clothing range, motivational speaker and board member at Leicester RFC.

Name: Rory Underwood
Born: 19th June 1963, Middlesbrough
Home Union: England
Position: Wing
Height / Weight: 5'8" (1.73m) / 190lbs (86kg)
Lions Tours: Australia (1989), New Zealand (1993)
Number of Tests: 6
Points: 4

Uttley

Uttley played for Fylde, Gosforth and then London Wasps, and also worked as a physical training instructor at Harrow. He won the first of his 23 England caps in 1973 and would go on to captain the side five times. He was also a member of the victorious Lions team that went undefeated in the four-Test series in South Africa in 1974.

Originally selected as a lock, he played in one of the most formidable back-row combinations ever assembled alongside Fergus Slattery and Mervyn Davies. They dominated the Springbok forwards and starved them of ball, which was the key to winning the series.

Uttley joined the Lions in 1989 as an assistant coach and the side duly delivered the Test series against Australia. Alongside Geoff Cooke, the pair guided England to Grand Slams in 1991 and 1992, and the 1991 Rugby World Cup final where an ill-advised change of tactics to an open running game saw them beaten by Australia.

He became the caretaker England manager in 1997 before handing the day-to-day reins to Clive Woodward in time for the disastrous Tour of Hell, during which the side suffered a record defeat to Australia and further losses to New Zealand and South Africa. He was dismissed by the RFU in 1999 by new chief executive Francis Baron and there's no doubt that the England setup missed his dedication and tactical nous during that year's World Cup.

The former President of the Sparks charity and member of the Wooden Spoon Society that helps disadvantaged children retired in 2008.

Above: *Roger Uttley (left) and Clive Woodward hold the English Rose during a press conference to announce the new England Coach*

Name: Roger Miles Uttley, OBE
Born: 11th September 1949, Blackpool
Home Union: England
Position: Lock, Flanker
Height / Weight: 6'4" (1.93m) / 213lbs (97kg)
Lions Tours: South Africa (1974), and as assistant coach: Australia (1989)
Number of Tests: 4
Points: 4

VICKERY

Vickery

Right: England's prop and captain Phil Vickery offloads the ball

Vickery was England's premier tight-head prop for more than a decade and his service to club and country saw him appointed captain by Brian Ashton in the build-up to the 2007 Six Nations. The side was still in transition after the high of the 2003 World Cup win and the low of the subsequent Six Nations disasters so Vickery was clearly going to be tested. He rose to the challenge, however, and led England to the 2007 World Cup final.

Vickery made his international debut as a relative novice against Wales in 1998, and he then endured the baptism of fire on the notorious Tour of Hell. Just a year later he was firmly established in the Woodward side but the 1999 World Cup campaign was a disappointment. Two years later he was called up for the Lions and he played in all three Tests against the Wallabies, although the tourists fell agonizingly short of a series win.

He was given the England captaincy on a low-key tour to Argentina and was then one of the rocks on which England's World Cup triumph was founded. He played in every game and scored his first international try against Samoa after a deft sidestep. A spate of injuries saw his appearances for Gloucester and England decline so he moved to Wasps and won the Heineken Cup in 2008. The following year he was on Lions duty again but he was obliterated in the first Test by Springbok prop Tendai

'The Beast' Mtawarira. He was dropped for the second Test but injuries to Gethin Jenkins and Adam Jones saw the 'Raging Bull' recalled for a consolation victory in the Johannesburg Test.

More injuries kept him out of the England frame in 2010 but he returned for the disappointing 2011 World Cup, after which he retired on medical grounds. In late 2011 he joined National League One side Cinderford as a coaching consultant.

Name: Philip John Vickery, MBE
Born: 14th March 1976, Barnstaple
Home Union: England
Position: Prop
Height / Weight: 6'3" (1.90m) / 275lbs (123kg)
Lions Tours: Australia (2001), South Africa (2009)
Number of Tests: 5
Points: 0

Wheeler

A n outspoken commentator on the RFU and vocal supporter of professionalism, Wheeler was arguably England's greatest hooker. His superb technique, ball-winning skills and powerful charges up the midfield, combined with great attacking vision, were the foundations for the England and Lions teams throughout the late 1970s.

Wheeler made his first appearance in a Leicester jersey in 1969 but he had to wait six years before making his England debut against France. He suffered a serious neck injury in his second international and missed the rest of the season but he was back to his best in 1976 – a year that included a demolition job on Australia – and was a regular fixture in the side until his retirement in 1984.

He was asked to standby as a possible replacement during the 1974 Lions tour to South Africa but in the end he wasn't required. He was selected for the 1977 trip to New Zealand but he only played in the second Test. A good win in Christchurch saw him retain his place but the tour was particularly gruelling and the Lions weren't quite good enough.

He captained Leicester for three years (1979-81) and led them to John Player Cups each season, but his finest hour in an international jersey came in 1980 when England won the Grand Slam. He was the first-choice hooker on the subsequent Lions tour to South Africa

and played in all four Tests. Despite another excellent tour for him personally, the Lions lost the series. The following year he was a member of the Barbarians' squad that won the Hong Kong Sevens.

He was finally given the England captaincy in 1983 and he immediately inspired them to a rare win over New Zealand. Wheeler retired following the 1984 Five Nations but he then played a key role in the transition from amateurism to professionalism. He is still chief executive at Leicester.

Above: *Peter Wheeler of England competes for the ball during a Five Nations Championship match*

Name: Peter John Wheeler
Born: 26th November 1948
Home Union: England
Position: Hooker
Height / Weight: 5'11" (1.80m) / 198lbs (90kg)
Lions Tours: New Zealand (1977), South Africa (1980)
Number of Tests: 7
Points: 0

Wilkinson

There's no doubt that New Zealand's Dan Carter and England's Jonny Wilkinson are the finest fly-halves of the current generation. Wilkinson, of course, will forever be remembered as the man whose drop-goal in the dying minutes of the 2003 World Cup gave England the Webb Ellis Trophy for the first time.

Wilkinson was assured of his place in the pantheon of England legends long before that incredible night, however. His prolific ability with the boot ensured that the young lad from Frimley broke club records at almost every age group. Pierrepont School led to Lord Wandsworth College and Durham University but he gave up his studies to join Newcastle Falcons. He made his England debut at 18, but it was an inauspicious start because his first two matches were followed by the infamous Tour of Hell to Australia in which the national side was thumped 76-0 by the hosts.

Wilkinson bounced back before the 1999 World Cup but some confusing selections by Clive Woodward meant he was only on the bench for the crucial quarter-final against South Africa. Janie de Beer kicked the Springboks to victory and Wilkinson didn't feature. In 2000 and 2001 he enhanced his reputation with solid kicking displays in the Six Nations and victory over the Springboks in Bloemfontein.

He was promptly selected for the 2001 Lions tour to Australia and helped the side to a big win in the first Test, but it was his risky pass that gifted Joe Roff a score in the second, which proved to be the turning point in the series. The Lions lost the decisive rubber despite Wilkinson scoring 18 points in the match.

His annus mirablis was 2003, of course, when he was instrumental in England's Grand Slam, their successful tour of Australia and New Zealand, and the World Cup triumph. He was

picked by Woodward for the 2005 Lions but he was ineffective against New Zealand and missed the final Test through injury. Injuries plagued much of his career thereafter and he didn't pull on the white jersey for four years (2003-07), although he did return for England's heroic run to the 2007 World Cup final.

In his short career he scored more than double the points of any other Englishman, and his 89 in the 2001 Six Nations championship is also a record. The British public voted him BBC Sports Personality of the Year in 2003. He remains the second highest points scorer in Test history (behind Carter) and although he has retired from international rugby he still plays domestically for Toulon.

Name: Jonathan Peter 'Jonny' Wilkinson, OBE
Born: 25th May 1979, Frimley, Surrey
Home Union: England
Position: Fly-half
Height / Weight: 5'10" (1.78m) / 196lbs (89kg)
Lions Tours: Australia (2001), New Zealand (2005)
Number of Tests: 6
Points: 67

Williams, Bleddyn

When Lions captain Karl Mullen was injured on the eve of the third Test against New Zealand in 1950, the tourists turned to Bleddyn Williams as his replacement. He was already Mullen's vice-captain and had been given the job of out-thinking the hosts tactically. He was perhaps the most complete centre of his generation and the flair player in the midfield.

Every centre needs the right attributes and the Welshman was blessed with quick and accurate hands, a sidestep off both feet, solid defence, and great positional awareness, which he later shared as a respected rugby correspondent. Williams's skills had already brought him to the attention of Cardiff and Wales when the Lions came calling. He teamed up with club-mate Jack Matthews and the pairing proved irresistible on the 1950 tour to New Zealand and Australia.

He was injured for the first Test but he recovered and played 20 of the team's 29 matches, scoring 13 tries, including one in the victory over Australia in the first Test. He then captained the Lions in the third and fourth Tests in New Zealand, although the tourists came up just short in both, particularly the decisive final match in which Williams was denied the

winning score by Peter Henderson.

He did finally beat the All Blacks with both Cardiff and Wales in 1953. He retired in 1955 with 27 international caps and 24 points to his name, a true rugby legend for club, country and the Lions.

Name: Bleddyn Williams, MBE
Born: 22nd February 1923, Taff's Well
Died: 6th July 2009
Home Union: Wales
Position: Centre
Height / Weight: 5'10" (1.78m) / 182lbs / 83kg)
Lions Tours: Australia & New Zealand (1950)
Number of Tests: 5
Points: 3

Williams, JJ

The Lions tours of 1974 and 1977 highlighted the northern hemisphere's technique and forward power and they also introduced the south to one of the sport's great finishers, Welsh wing JJ Williams. He had represented his country in the short sprints at the 1970 Commonwealth Games but, by 1974, he was focusing on rugby.

In only his second top-flight season the 26-year-old schoolteacher took unpaid leave to tour South Africa, but his 12 tries from as many games and four in the Test series immediately brought him to the attention of planet rugby. Pace may have been his primary weapon but speed alone is not enough when up against the best cover and rush defences. He soon developed a delicate kick and chase, slick hands, and a penchant for attacking the blindside with scrum-half Gareth Edwards. Against a South West Districts XV, he equalled David Duckham's record of six tries in a game. He scored again in the second and third Tests to help seal the series win.

Three years later, Williams toured New Zealand, although his trip was curtailed by a hamstring injury in the third Test. By then he'd already scored 10 tries, however, this despite poor weather and dreadful pitches nullifying his trademark chip and chase. He was again on hand to touch down in the second Test after a brilliant dummy.

He retired from international rugby in 1979 with 30 caps and 12 tries to his name and now runs a commercial painting company.

Above: *Welsh rugby union player John J Williams*

Name: John James 'JJ' Williams, MBE
Born: 1st April 1948, Maesteg
Home Union: Wales
Position: Wing
Height / Weight: 5'9" (1.75m) / 163lbs (74kg)
Lions Tours: South Africa (1974), Australia & New Zealand (1977)
Number of Tests: 7
Points: 20

Williams, JPR

The attacking full-back role may have been developed by Ken Scotland in the 1950s, but it was JPR who turned it into an art form during the early 1970s. Williams was a superb all-round sportsman who won a junior tennis tournament in 1966. He decided to concentrate on rugby, however, and moved to London Welsh in 1968. He made his debut for Wales the following year and made such an impression that he was selected for the Lions in 1971, where he proved himself the tourists' best number 15.

Fearless in the tackle, secure under the high ball, and devastating in attack, JPR also had a precision kicking game (in attack and defence) and he was particularly effective when exploiting the opposition's tactical inadequacies. In fact every kick he returned seemed to go back with interest, but he knew keeping the ball in play was more important that looking for touch because it kept the attacking options open. He hit the line with such pace that the opposition was immediately on the back foot, and the timing of his passes and his general creativity usually split any unprepared defences.

Williams never shirked physical confrontation and in 1974 he had to be restrained by the police when tangling with Springbok great Tommy Bedford. In all, he made 30 appearances for the Lions, including eight Test matches. He scored 16 points in 1971 and 12 in 1974, which included five tries. And he sealed the 1971 series with a rare 50-yard drop-goal in the fourth Test.

He finally retired in 1981 with 55 Welsh caps and 36 points under his belt. He continued his career as an orthopaedic surgeon and didn't retire from club rugby until 2003. He is now an ambassador for the sport, a true Welsh rugby legend.

Name: John Peter Rhys 'JPR' Williams, MBE
Born: 2nd March 1949, Cardiff
Home Union: Wales
Position: Full-back
Height / Weight: 6'1" (1.85m) / 190lbs (86kg)
Lions Tours: New Zealand (1971), South Africa (1974)
Number of Tests: 8
Points: 3

Williams, Rhys

Right: *Rhys Williams (centre, rear) during a team photo shoot*

Williams was educated at grammar school and Cardiff University, where he gained a reputation as a fine second-row forward. He made his debut for Llanelli aged 19 and went on to captain the side in the late 1950s. He also played for the RAF having qualified as an education officer.

He collected his first Wales cap against Ireland in the 1954 Five Nations, and he was then selected to tour with the Lions to South Africa the following year. It was a successful tour and the Lions shared the Test series against a strong Springbok outfit. Four years later Williams toured again, this time to Australia and New Zealand. In the final Test he took six consecutive lineouts to deny the hosts a chance at squaring the match, and he was then voted player of the series.

In all he played in ten consecutive Tests for the tourists, winning two against South Africa, two against Australia and one against the All Blacks. His presence in the scrum, power in the loose and ability to win vital ball at the restart and lineout sees Williams repeatedly voted into the all-time Welsh team.

Name: Rhys Haydn Williams
Born: 14th July 1930, Cwmllynfell
Died: 27th January 1993, Whitchurch
Home Union: Wales
Position: Lock
Height / Weight: 6'3" (1.91m) / 234lbs (106kg)
Lions Tours: South Africa (1955), Australia & New Zealand (1959)
Number of Tests: 10
Points: 0

Williams, Shane

Below: *Shane Williams of Wales breaks away*

Williams is one of the most devastating finishers in the game. Slight of build but nimble of foot and with electrifying pace over short distances, he has left many of the best defences clutching thin air.

His size led some to doubt him in his early career, and a spate of injuries threatened to derail his ascent to greatness, but he made his debut in 2000. More injury problems and general apathy from the Welsh coaching panel saw him sidelined until 2003 but he returned in time to claim a place at that year's World Cup. He lit up the tournament and finally silenced his critics with his lightning breaks, competence under the high ball and several huge performances, notably against New Zealand and England albeit in losing causes.

Williams scored the crucial try against England and was omnipresent in the Grand Slam-winning Welsh side of 2005. This earned him a call-up to the Lions squad, but he only played in one Test in New Zealand and the tourists were soundly beaten. He was back to his brilliant best during the 2007 World Cup when he scored six tries, including a magnificent solo effort against Fiji. After another Grand Slam

Below: Shane Williams of Wales breaks away

the following season, he was voted IRB Player of the Year and the Lions came calling again in 2009. He was underused due to a slight dip in form but he still scored twice in the Lions' consolation victory.

Injury ruled him out of the 2011 Six Nations but Williams returned for the World Cup and helped Wales to fourth place in what was a magnificent tournament for him and the team. He made his final Test appearance against Australia in December 2011, capping an outstanding international career with a try.

Williams will be remembered as one of the best wingers in world rugby. His flat speed, wicked sidestep and eye for a gap endeared him to fans and more than compensated for his slightly shaky defence. Attacking rugby had been the hallmark of all the great Welsh teams and Williams brought his flair and excitement to a new generation. He bowed out with 91 international appearances and 60 tries to his name, placing him third on the all-time list. He retired in 2012 to take up a backroom role with the Ospreys.

> **Name:** Shane Mark Williams, MBE
> **Born:** 26th February 1977, Swansea
> **Home Union:** Wales
> **Position:** Wing
> **Height / Weight:** 5'7" (1.70m) / 176lbs (80kg)
> **Lions Tours:** New Zealand (2005), South Africa (2009)
> **Number of Tests:** 4
> **Points:** 10

Windsor

Willie John McBride may have had his hand on the tiller during the Lions tour to South Africa in 1974, but few of his foot soldiers encapsulated the winning mentality more than hooker Bobby Windsor. The Pontypool steelworker brought a mix of technical excellence, raw courage and outright aggression that lifted the entire squad on their way to series victory.

'The Duke', as his team-mates liked to call the former outside half, was taught by the great coach Ray Prosser, but he was still a somewhat surprising choice to join the Lions given that he'd only just started playing for Wales. Whether he listened to the doubters or not is unknown but he knuckled down and forced his way into the Test side ahead of Ken Kennedy.

Windsor was one of the characters of the touring party and was soon selling excess kit to raise cash. On the pitch he was combative and courageous in the face of the big Springbok forwards, but he was also an asset in the loose with his quick hands and hard tackling. With Fran Cotton and Ian McLauchlan on either side, the trio of pocket-battleships sank the Springbok pack.

By 1977, Windsor was playing in a front row for Pontypool and Wales that included Charlie Faulkner and Graham Price. This new forward line, known as the 'Viet-Gwent' travelled to New Zealand and dominated the provincial

Above: *Bobby Windsor (centre) about to hit the scrum machine*

sides, although, possibly to the side's detriment, they were not given the Test berths and the series was lost. Price played in all four internationals but Faulkner was kept out by Cotton, and Windsor was controversially dropped after the first Test for Peter Wheeler.

Windsor retired from international rugby in 1979 and finally published his autobiography, The Iron Duke, in 2010.

Name: Bobby Windsor
Born: 31st January 1948, Newport
Home Union: Wales
Position: Hooker
Height / Weight: 5'9" (1.75m) / 205lbs (93kg)
Lions Tours: South Africa (1974), New Zealand (1977)
Number of Tests: 5
Points: 0

Winterbottom

Peter Winterbottom began his rugby career as a No.8 for Lancashire schools and England colts, but he switched to flanker in the England B setup in 1981. His hard work, aggression and durability endeared him to the coaches and he made his England debut a year later in a historic win over Australia at Twickenham. Erica Roe's streak made the occasion even more memorable.

Winterbottom left Headingley for Hawkes Bay in New Zealand where he honed his handling skills and earned a reputation as a hard man in the mold of legendary French flanker Jean-Pierre Rives. Winterbottom continued his England career throughout the rather bleak if brutal 1980s and he was the first forward to reach 50 caps, leading Brian Moore to describe him as the hardest man he ever met.

He toured New Zealand with the 1983 Lions and played in all four Tests. Despite losing the series, Winterbottom was voted one of the players of the season. The World Cup in 1987 was another low point but,

domestically at least, he could do no wrong, a move to Harlequins bringing him three Pilkington Cup finals, although he only won one (against Northampton in 1991).

The 1990s saw England's fortunes improve under the leadership of coach Geoff Cooke and captain Will Carling, and Winterbottom was ever-present in the Grand Slam sides of 1991 and 1992. Losing to Australia in the 1991 World Cup final was another bitter pill but Winterbottom was as durable in spirit as he was in body and he didn't retire from the international stage until he'd won a majority verdict over the peerless Michael Jones on the 1993 Lions tour to New Zealand.

Winterbottom didn't wait to be dropped so he retired at the peak of his game and he is still rated as one of the best flankers in the world. He is now a respected international financier.

Name: Peter James Winterbottom
Born: 31st May 1960, Otley, West Yorkshire
Home Union: England
Position: Flanker
Height / Weight: 6'0" (1.83m) / 207lbs (94kg)
Lions Tours: Australia (1989), New Zealand (1993)
Number of Tests: 7
Points: 0

Wood

Wood began his career with Garryowen, helping them to all-Ireland titles in 1992 and 1994 before joining Harlequins. He proved himself a versatile, mobile, powerful, try-scoring hooker and, having already cemented his place in the national team, earned selection for the 1997 Lions tour to South Africa.

His contribution to the score that won the series for the tourists summed up his unorthodox style. His throw-in to the lineout was unexceptional but it was his break down the blindside and kick to the Springbok corner that had the hosts scrambling to defend a position from which they conceded territory. The Lions duly secured possession and Guscott kicked the decisive drop-goal. It was this added dimension that gave the Lions the edge and he was on hand again during the 2001 tour to Australia, a year in which he was voted the IRB Player of the Year.

His performances leading up to the tour saw him vie for the captaincy with Martin Johnson but, despite losing out to the Englishman, he remained a central influence on the team's fortunes and morale. He skippered the side against Western Australia in Perth and was the key man in the front row during the Test series. Never lacking in confidence, he even went for an outrageous 50-yard drop-goal in the first match.

Wood retired from international rugby after a disappointing exit to France in the 2003 World Cup. His record as a player is impressive: 58 Ireland caps and 15 tries (a world record for a hooker), with five caps for the Lions on two tours. He now works for the BBC and The Daily Telegraph as an informed and articulate commentator on the game he graced.

Name: Keith Gerard Mallinson Wood
Born: 27th January 1972, Killaloe
Home Union: Ireland
Position: Hooker
Height / Weight: 6'0" (1.83m) / 234lbs (106kg)
Lions Tours: South Africa (1997), Australia (2001)
Number of Tests: 5
Points: 0

Young

Young was a mobile but combative prop who would eventually play both rugby codes at the highest level for more than 18 years. He was called up by Wales during the 1987 Rugby World Cup when Stuart Evans was ruled out (he happened to be playing his club rugby in Australia and was able to join the team immediately).

Two years later he played in all three Tests for the Lions against Australia, and it was his abrasive approach upfront that helped starve the Wallabies of quick ball. When he returned to the UK he was snapped up by Leeds rugby league in a lucrative deal but he soon switched to Salford. He represented Wales in the 13-man code before returning to union in 1996. The following year he was again chosen to join the Lions in South Africa, although he didn't make the Test side. He toured with the team for a third time in Australia in 2001 but he was again a midweek player rather than a Test candidate. He retired from international rugby in 2002 after racking up 51 union caps and 14 league caps for Wales.

His club career was far from over, however. He joined Cardiff Blues in 2003 and coached the side to a Heineken Cup semi-final and the Anglo-Welsh title in 2009. He was also at the tiller when the Blues became the first Welsh provincial side to claim a European title. In 2011, Young left the Blues and took over as Director of Rugby with Premiership heavyweights London Wasps.

Above: David 'Dai' Young was a giant in both rugby codes

Name: David 'Dai' Young	
Born: 26th July 1967, Aberdare	
Home Union: Wales	
Position: Prop	
Height / Weight: 6'2" (1.88m) / 259lbs (117kg)	
Lions Tours: Australia (1989), South Africa (1997), Australia (2001)	
Number of Tests: 3	
Points: 0	

The Lions in Australia 2013
The Complete Story of the Lions Tour

Ian Robertson and Mick Cleary combine to tell the full story of the Lions tour in a book that wil be published within days of the last Test Match in Sydney

Over 100 photographs capturing the great moments on and off the pitch in 160 pages plus a full statistical summary of the tour

£20 RRP   978 1 85291 155 7

Lennard Publishing
distributed by G2 Entertainment

ALSO IN THIS SERIES

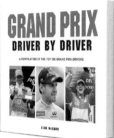

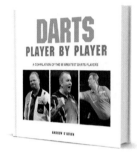

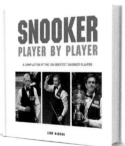

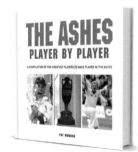

**The pictures in this book were provided
courtesy of the following:**

GETTY IMAGES
101 Bayham Street, London NW1 0AG

WIKICOMMONS
commons.wikimedia.org

Design & Artwork by: Scott Giarnese & Alex Young

Published by: Demand Media Limited & G2 Entertainment Limited

Publishers: Jason Fenwick & Jules Gammond

Written by Liam McCann